D ... UR ... Y

Barbara Taylor and Mark O'Shea
Consultant: Dr Richard A Griffiths

This edition is published by Southwater

13314548

Southwater is an imprint of Anness Publishing Ltd
Hermes House, 88–89 Blackfriars Road, London SE1 8HA
tel. 020 7401 2077; fax 020 7633 9499
www.southwaterbooks.com; info@anness.com

UK agent: The Manning Partnership Ltd, 6 The Old Dairy,
Melcombe Road, Bath BA2 3LR; tel. 01225 478444; fax 01225 478440;
sales@manning-partnership.co.uk

UK distributor: Grantham Book Services Ltd, Isaac Newton Way,
Alma Park Industrial Estate, Grantham, Lincs NG31 9SD;
tel. 01476 541080; fax 01476 541061; orders@gbs.tbs-ltd.co.uk

North American agent/distributor: National Book Network,
4501 Forbes Boulevard, Suite 200, Lanham, MD 20706;
tel. 301 459 3366; fax 301 429 5746; www.nbnbooks.com

Australian agent/distributor: Pan Macmillan Australia,
Level 18, St Martins Tower, 31 Market St, Sydney, NSW 2000;
tel. 1300 135 113; fax 1300 135 103; customer.service@macmillan.com.au

New Zealand agent/distributor: David Bateman Ltd, 30 Tarndale Grove,
Off Bush Road, Albany, Auckland; tel. (09) 415 7664; fax (09) 415 8892

A CIP catalogue record for this book is available from the British Library.

Publisher: Joanna Lorenz
Editorial Director: Judith Simons
Project Editors: Nicole Pearson, Joy Wotton and Elizabeth Woodland
Copy Editors: Daniel Gilpin, Peter Harrison and Charlotte Hurdman
Designers: Linda Penny, Ann Samuel and Rita Wuthrich
Jacket Design: Alix Wood
Illustrators: Linden Artists, Stuart Lafford and Vanessa Card
Picture Researchers: Su Alexander and Wendy Wilders
Prepress Controller: Neil McLaren
Production Controller: Darren Price

Previously published in two separate
volumes, *Nature Watch: Crocodiles* and
Nature Watch: Lizards

10 9 8 7 6 5 4 3 2 1

CONTENTS

INTRODUCTION

For over 150 million years, a group of reptiles called the dinosaurs ruled the Earth. They developed into over 1,000 different kinds, including long-necked giants, terrifying predators and armored, horned and duck-billed dinosaurs. Living alongside the dinosaurs all those millions of years ago were other reptiles, including early lizards and crocodiles. Some of these crocodiles were powerful enough to attack the biggest dinosaurs. All the dinosaurs died out 65 million years ago, but some of the small, flesh-eating dinosaurs may have developed into birds. Crocodiles are probably more closely related to birds than they are to lizards and snakes.

The name "dinosaur" means "terrible lizard" because dinosaurs looked rather like giant lizards. Like all reptiles, they had a bony skeleton and scaly skin, and laid eggs with shells. Yet dinosaurs moved in a different way from lizards and other living reptiles. They walked with straight legs tucked under their bodies, not sprawled out to the sides like a lizard or a crocodilian. This allowed them to move faster, walk farther and grow bigger than other reptiles. Many dinosaurs walked on two long back legs and the smaller ones whizzed around at high speed. Lizards and crocodilians walk on all fours, although some lizards can lift the front half of their bodies off the ground and run on two legs for short distances. Crocodilians are not speedy creatures normally but can occasionally put on a surprising turn of speed to catch prey or escape danger. Their large, powerful tail propels them through the water with effortless ease and they also toboggan quickly over muddy riverbanks by sliding on their bellies.

▲ **FAST LIZARDS**
Basilisks have long tails, eyelids, four legs and their bodies are covered with overlapping scales. Their long hind legs have fringed scales on the outer toes, which help them to walk on water. They can only do this at great speed, because when they start to slow down, they break through the surface of the water and have to swim.

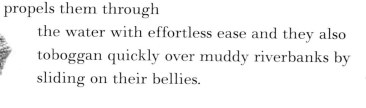

◄ **CHAMELEON HUNTERS**
Chameleons stalk their insect prey carefully, gripping twigs and branches firmly with their curly toes and tail.

The tough, scaly body armor of crocodilians and their large size as adults make them difficult for most predators to attack. Lizards, on the other hand, tend to be small, rather fragile reptiles, which are constantly in danger of attack. They need to be able to move fast to stay alive. A flexible backbone allows lizards to move easily as they get into their stride. Some lizards are expert tree climbers or glide from branch to branch on "wings" of outstretched skin.

▼ ON THE MOVE
Crocodilians swim easily and gracefully in the water but often look slow and clumsy on land.

Most lizards and all crocodilians are carnivores, hunting living prey but also taking advantage of wounded, sick or dying animals and scavenging from the carcasses of dead animals. They have a strong sense of smell and can detect the smell of food from up to 2½ miles away. Some carnivorous dinosaurs, such as *Tyrannosaurus rex*, are also thought to have had an excellent sense of smell. This would have helped them to track down dying prey or carcasses. Unlike crocodiles and most modern lizards, a lot of dinosaurs ate plants. There were about thirty times more plant-eating dinosaurs than meat-eating ones. Plant-eating reptiles are rare, and only tortoises and a few lizards and turtles have a vegetarian diet. Most plant-eating lizards eat leaves, but some snack on fruit, seeds or flowers. The marine iguana is an unusual lizard that eats seaweed. One dinosaur, *Iguanodon*, was named after the iguana.

Some dinosaurs were thought to be good parents, guarding their nests and young. Some young dinosaurs, such as *Triceratops*, may also have been protected by the adults in a herd, like baby elephants are today. Lizard mothers do not usually protect their eggs, but some lizards give birth to live young and a few protect their babies for a short time. Crocodilians show more parental care, with mothers often guarding the nest and eggs from predators (such as monitor lizards) and sometimes helping the eggs to hatch. Mother crocodilians may also gently carry their young from the nest to the water in their mouths and guard them while they are small. Young crocodilians usually stay together for a while in a noisy group called a pod, helping to warn each other of danger and calling to nearby adults for help when they are in distress. Adult crocodilians also gather in loose groups from time to time, for activities such as sharing food, basking in the sun and nesting. They communicate with a variety of sounds, smells and body language.

▶ STICKY FEET
Geckos, such as this Frilled leaf-tail, have big, padded toes. The hairs on their feet, called setea, allow them to grip to any surface, wet or dry. The tips of their feet are so sticky that they can hang with all their weight suspended by a single toe.

CROCODILIANS

Crocodilians are the most advanced of all living reptiles, with keen senses and a well-developed brain. These armor-plated predators are superbly adapted for life in warm rivers, lakes, marshes and swamps. They swim well, catch food in their powerful jaws and are well protected from predators when they reach adult size. Big crocodiles can even survive for up to two years between meals.

What is a Crocodilian?

Crocodilians are scaly, armor-clad reptiles that include crocodiles, alligators, caimans and gharials. They are survivors from a prehistoric age—their relatives first lived on the earth with the dinosaurs nearly 200 million years ago. Today, they are the dinosaurs' closest living relatives, apart from birds.

Crocodilians are fierce predators. They lurk motionless in rivers, lakes and swamps, waiting to snap up prey with their enormous jaws and strong teeth. Their prey ranges from insects, frogs and fish to birds and large mammals, such as deer and zebras. Very few crocodilians regularly attack and kill humans. Most are timid. Crocodilians usually live in warm, tropical places in or near freshwater, and some live in the sea. They hunt and feed mainly in the water, but crawl onto dry land to sunbathe, build nests and lay their eggs.

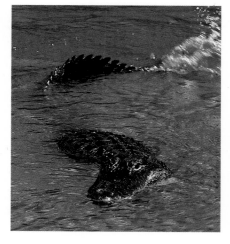

▲ SCALY TAILS
Like many crocodilians, an American alligator uses its long, strong tail to swim through the water. The tail moves from side to side to push the alligator along. The tail is the same length as the rest of the body.

long, strong tail has flat sides to push aside water for swimming

► CROCODILIAN CHARACTERISTICS
With its thick, scaly skin, huge jaws and powerful tail, this American alligator looks like a living dinosaur. Its eyes and nostrils are on top of its head so that it can see and breathe when the rest of its body is underwater. On land, crocodilians slither along on their bellies, but they can lift themselves up on their four short legs to walk.

The Chinese Dragon
People in China have worshiped the dragon, a mythical creature, for centuries. The original stories surrounding the dragon may have been based on the real-life Chinese alligator. According to ancient texts, the dragon was a supernatural creature that could take on many different forms. It could change instantly from thick to thin or long to short, and could soar into the heavens or plunge to the depths of the sea.

▲ TALKING HEADS

Huge, powerful jaws lined with sharp teeth make Nile crocodiles killing machines. They are some of the world's largest and most dangerous reptiles. The teeth are used to attack and grip prey, but are useless for chewing. Prey has to be swallowed whole or in chunks.

► SHUTEYE

Although this spectacled caiman has its eyes shut, it is probably not asleep, but dozing. Two butterflies are basking in safety on the caiman's head. Predators will not dare attack it because the caiman is still sensitive to what is going on around it, even though its eyes are shut.

► SOAKING UP THE SUN

Nile crocodiles sun themselves on a sandbank. This is called basking and warms the body. Crocodilians are cold-blooded, which means that their body temperature is affected by their surroundings. They have no fur or feathers to keep them warm, nor can they shiver to warm up. They move in and out of the water to warm up or cool down.

Scales on the back are usually much more bony than those on the belly

scaly skin covers the whole body for protection and camouflage

Did you know? Most crocodilians live for about 50 years but some live up to 100.

eyes and nostrils on top of the head

Digits (toes) of each foot are slightly webbed

American alligator *(Alligator mississippiensis)*

long snout with sharp teeth to catch prey

9

Croc or Gator?

There are 13 species (kinds) of crocodile, two species of alligator, six species of caiman, and two species of gharial. Gharials have distinctive long, slender snouts, but crocodiles and alligators are often more difficult to tell apart. Crocodiles usually have longer, more pointed snouts than alligators. Crocodiles also have one very large tooth sticking up from each side of the bottom jaw when they close their mouths.

▲ CAIMAN EYES
Most caimans have bonier ridges between their eyes than alligators. These ridges help strengthen the skull and look like glasses people wear to help them see. Caimans are usually smaller than alligators.

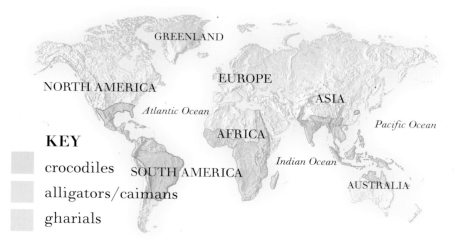

KEY
crocodiles
alligators/caimans
gharials

▲ WHERE IN THE WORLD?
Crocodiles are the most widespread crocodilian and live in Central and South America, Africa, southern Asia and Australia. Caimans live in Central and South America, while alligators live in the southeastern United States and China. The gharial is found in southern Asia, while the false gharial lives in Southeast Asia.

▼ A CROCODILE'S SMILE
With its mouth closed, a crocodile's fourth tooth in the lower jaw fits into a notch on the outside of the upper jaw. No teeth can be seen on the bottom jaw of an alligator's closed mouth.

Chinese alligator
(*Alligator sinensis*)

▲ COOL ALLIGATOR
There are two species of alligator, the Chinese alligator (*shown above*) and the American alligator. Alligators are the only crocodilians that can survive cooler temperatures and live outside the tropics.

▶ DIFFERENT SNOUTS

Crocodilian snouts are different shapes and sizes because of the food they eat and the way they live. Gharials and crocodiles have narrow, pointy snouts suited to eating fish. Alligators and caimans have wider, rounder snouts that can manage larger prey, such as birds and mammals. Their jaws are strong enough to overpower victims that are even larger than they are.

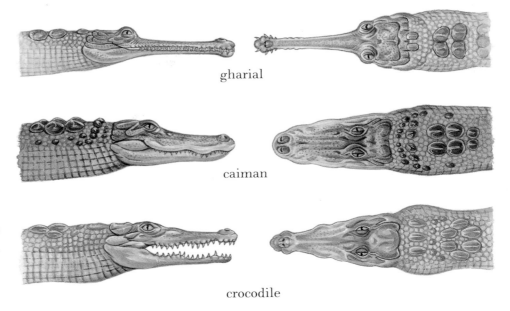

gharial

caiman

crocodile

◀ OUT TO SEA

The enormous saltwater crocodile, often called the saltie, has the largest range of all the crocodilians. It is found from the east coast of India through Southeast Asia to the Philippines, New Guinea and northern Australia. Saltwater crocodiles are one of the few species found far out to sea, but they do live in freshwater rivers and lakes as well.

▶ POT NOSE

Two species of gharial, the gharial, or gavial, and the false gharial, live in the rivers, lakes and swamps of southern Asia. The name comes from the bump on the nose of the male gharial, which is called a ghara (pot) in the Hindi language. Some experts say the false gharial is a species of crocodile and is therefore not really part of the gharial family.

adult male gharials have a conspicuous bump at the tip of their snouts

gharial
(*Gavialis gangeticus*)

Large and Small

Can you imagine a crocodile that weighs as much as three cars? A big, 23-foot-long saltwater crocodile is as heavy as this. It is the heaviest living reptile in the world. Other enormous crocodilians include Nile crocodiles, gharials and American alligators, which can reach lengths of 18 feet or more. Very large crocodiles and alligators are now rare because many are hunted and killed for their meat and skins before they grow to their maximum size. The smallest species of crocodilian are the dwarf caimans of South America and the African dwarf crocodile. These forest-dwelling reptiles grow to about 5 feet long.

▲ **BIGGEST CAIMAN**
The black caiman is the largest of the caimans. It can grow to over 19 ft long and is the biggest predator in South America. Black caimans live in the flooded Amazon forest, around lakes and slow-flowing rivers. They hunt at night for capybaras, turtles, deer and fish.

▲ **A CROC IN EACH HAND**
A person holds a baby Orinoco crocodile (*top*) and a baby spectacled caiman (*bottom*). As adults, the Orinoco crocodile will be twice the length of the caiman, reaching about 16 ft. You can clearly see how the crocodile has a longer, thinner snout than the caiman.

Crocodile God
The ancient Egyptians worshiped the crocodile-headed god Sebek. He was the god of lakes and rivers, and is shown here with Pharaoh Amenhotep III. A shrine to Sebek was built at Shedet. Here, a Nile crocodile decorated with gold rings and bracelets lived in a special pool. It was believed to be the living god. Other crocodiles were also treated with great respect and hand-fed on meat, cakes, milk and honey.

◄ SUPER-SNOUTED CROCODILE

The mugger crocodile of India and surrounding lands has the broadest snout of all crocodiles, making it look more like an alligator. Adult males reach about 13 ft long. The name mugger comes from its habit of snatching fish out of people's fishing nets.

◄ SMALLEST CROCODILIAN

Cuvier's dwarf caiman is about a fifth of the size of a giant saltwater crocodile, yet it would still only just fit on your bed! It lives in the rainforests of the Amazon basin in South America. It has particularly tough, armored skin to protect it from rocks in fast-flowing rivers. It has a short snout and high, smooth skull. Its short snout does not prevent it from eating a lot of fish.

Did you know? Male alligators keep growing until they are 15 years old.

► MONSTER CROC

The huge Nile crocodile is the biggest and strongest freshwater predator in Africa. It can grow up to 19 ft long and eats any prey it can overpower, including monkeys, antelopes, zebras and sometimes, people. Nile crocodiles probably kill at least 300 people a year in Africa. Despite its name, the Nile crocodile is not just found along the Nile but also lives in rivers, lakes and swamps through most of tropical Africa.

Scaly Skin

The outside of a crocodilian's body is completely covered in a suit of leathery armor. It is made up of rows of tough scales, called scutes, that are set into a thick layer of skin. Some scutes have small bony disks inside them. Most crocodilians have bony scutes only on their backs, but some, such as caimans, have them on their bellies as well. The tail never contains bony scutes, but it does have thicker tail scutes. As crocodilians grow, bigger scutes develop under the old ones. Crocodilians do not get rid of their old scaly skin in a big piece, like a snake, or in patches like a lizard. Old scutes drop off one at a time, just as humans lose flakes of skin all the time. On the head, the skin is fused directly to the bones of the skull without any muscles or fat in between.

Tricky Alligator
A Guyanese myth tells how the Sun was tricked by an alligator into letting him guard his fishponds from a thief. The thief was the alligator, and to punish him the Sun slashed his body, forming the scales. The alligator promised the Sun his daughter for a wife. He had no children, so he carved her from a tree. The Sun and the woman's offspring were the Carob people.

▲ **COLOR CHANGE**
Most crocodilians are brightly colored or patterned as babies, but these features usually fade as they grow older. They have more or less disappeared in fully-grown adults. The colors and patterns may help with camouflage by breaking up the outline of the body.

▲ **NECK ARMOR**
Heavy, bony scutes pack tightly together to create a rigid and formidable armor on the back and neck of an African dwarf crocodile. Even the scutes on the sides of its body and tail are heavily armored. This species lives in the dwindling rainforests of West and Central Africa. The small size and bony armor of the dwarf crocodile has saved it so far from being hunted for its skin.

14

▲ MISSING SCALES

The gharial has fewer rows of armored scutes along its back than other crocodilians. Adults have four rows of deeply ridged back scutes, whereas other crocodilians have two or four extra rows in the middle of the back. The scutes on the sides and belly are unarmored.

▲ BONY BACK

The belly of a saltwater crocodile does not have bony plates in the scutes. You can see the difference in this close-up. Large, bony back scutes are shown at the top of the picture, and the smaller, smoother belly scutes are at the bottom. The scutes are arranged in rows.

► EXTRA ARMOR

This close-up shows the skin of a dwarf caiman—the most heavily armored crocodilian. It has strong bones in the scutes on its belly as well as its back. This provides protection from predators. Even its eyelids are protected by bony plates.

Did you know? The scales of the black caiman are as tough as the heel of a boot.

► ALBINO ALLIGATOR

An albino crocodilian would not survive long in the wild. It does not blend in well with its surroundings, making it easy prey. Those born in captivity in zoos or crocodile farms may survive to adulthood. True albinos are white with pink eyes. White crocodilians with blue eyes are not true albinos.

American alligator (*Alligator mississippiensis*)

15

Bodies and Bones

The crocodilian body has changed very little over the last 200 million years. It is superbly adapted to life in the water. Crocodilians can breathe with just their nostrils above the surface. Underwater, ears and nostrils close, and a transparent third eyelid sweeps across the eye for protection. Crocodilians are the only reptiles with ear flaps. Inside the long, lizard-like body a bony skeleton supports and protects the lungs, heart, stomach and other soft organs. The stomach is in two parts, one for grinding food, the other for absorbing nutrients. Unlike other reptiles, whose hearts have only one to three chambers, a crocodilian's heart has four chambers, like a mammal's. This allows the heart to pump more oxygen-rich blood to the brain during a dive. The thinking part of its brain is more developed than in other reptiles. This enables a crocodilian to learn things rather than act only on instinct.

▲ **THROAT FLAP**

A crocodilian has no lips, so it is unable to seal its mouth underwater. Instead, two special flaps at the back of the throat keep water from filling the mouth and flowing into the lungs. This enables the crocodile to open its mouth underwater to catch and eat prey without drowning.

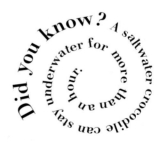

Did you know? A saltwater crocodile can stay underwater for more than an hour.

◄ **PREHISTORIC LOOKS**

These American alligators look much like their crocodilian ancestors that lived with the dinosaurs long ago. Crocodilians are the largest living reptiles. The heaviest is the saltwater crocodile which can reach up to 2,420 lbs.

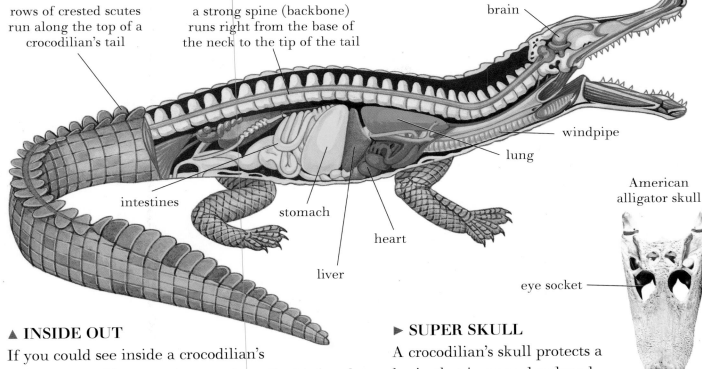

rows of crested scutes run along the top of a crocodilian's tail

a strong spine (backbone) runs right from the base of the neck to the tip of the tail

brain

windpipe

lung

intestines

stomach

heart

liver

American alligator skull

eye socket

American crocodile skull

▲ INSIDE OUT

If you could see inside a crocodilian's body you would see a mixture of reptile, bird and mammal features. The crocodilian's brain and shoulder blades are like a bird's. Its heart, diaphragm and efficient breathing system are similar to those of mammals. The stomach and digestive system are those of a reptile, as they deal with food that cannot be chewed.

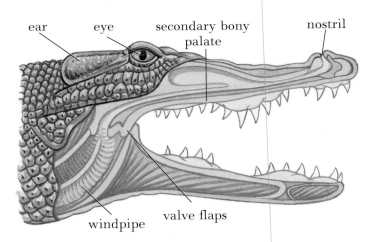

ear   eye   secondary bony palate   nostril

windpipe   valve flaps

▲ WELL-DESIGNED

A view inside the head of a crocodilian shows the ear, eye and nostril openings set high up in the skull. The bones in the mouth are joined together to create a secondary bony palate that separates the nostrils from the mouth. Flaps of skin form a valve, sealing off the windpipe underwater.

► SUPER SKULL

A crocodilian's skull protects a brain that is more developed than any other reptile's. The skull is wider and more rounded in alligators (*top*), and long and triangular in crocodiles (*bottom*). Behind the eye sockets are two large holes where jaw muscles attach to the skull.

► STOMACH STONES

Crocodilians swallow objects, such as pebbles, to help break down their food. These gastroliths (stomach stones) churn around inside

part of the stomach, helping to cut up food so it can be digested. Some very unusual gastroliths have been found, such as bottles, coins, a whistle and a thermos.

Jaws and Teeth

The mighty jaws of a crocodilian and its impressive rows of spiky teeth are lethal weapons for catching prey. Crocodilians have two or three times as many teeth as a human. The sharp, jagged teeth at the front of the mouth, called canines, are used to pierce and grip prey. The force of the jaws closing drives these teeth, like a row of knives, deep into a victim's flesh. The short, blunt molar teeth at the back of the mouth are used for crushing prey. Crocodilian teeth are useless for chewing food, and the jaws cannot be moved sideways to chew either. Food has to be swallowed whole, or torn into chunks. The teeth are constantly growing. If a tooth falls out, a new one grows through to replace it.

▲ MEGA JAWS

The jaws of a Nile crocodile close with tremendous force. They sink into their prey with tons of crushing pressure. Yet the muscles that open the jaws are weak. A thick rubber band over the snout can easily hold a crocodile's jaws shut.

◄ NEW TEETH FOR OLD

Each tooth is set in a socket and held in place by connective tissue. Throughout a crocodilian's life, the old teeth fall out and new teeth underneath take their place. Teeth last up to two years before falling out. Alternate teeth are replaced together, so that not all the teeth in one part of the mouth are lost at the same time.

◀ LOTS OF TEETH

The gharial has more teeth than any other crocodilian, around 110. Its teeth are also smaller than those of other crocodilians and are all the same size. The narrow, beak-like snout and long, thin teeth of the gharial are geared to grabbing fish with a sweeping sideways movement of the head. The sharp teeth interlock to trap and impale the slippery prey.

CHARMING

Crocodilian teeth are sometimes made into necklaces. People wear them as decoration or lucky charms. In South America, the Montana people of Peru believe they will be protected from poisoning by wearing a crocodile tooth.

▲ BABY TEETH

A baby American alligator is born with a full set of 80 teeth when it hatches from its egg. Baby teeth are not as sharp as adult teeth and are more fragile. They are like tiny needles. In young crocodiles, the teeth at the back of the mouth usually fall out first. In adults, it is the teeth at the front that are replaced more often.

▶ GRABBING TEETH

A Nile crocodile grasps a lump of prey ready for swallowing. If prey is too large to swallow whole, the crocodile grips the food firmly in its teeth and shakes its head hard so that any unwanted pieces are shaken off.

a Nile crocodile has 68 teeth lining its huge jaws

Did you know? A Nile crocodile may use 45 sets of teeth by the time it is 12 ft long.

On the Move

Have you ever seen a film of an alligator gliding through the water with slow, S-shaped sweeps of its powerful tail? Crocodilians move gracefully and easily in the water, using very little energy and keeping most of their body hidden under the surface. Legs lie close alongside bodies to make them streamlined, and cut down drag from the water. They may be used as rudders to change course. On land, the short legs of crocodilians make their walk look slow and clumsy, but they can move quite fast if they need to. Some can gallop at 11 miles per hour when running for short distances of up to 295 feet. Crocodilians also move by means of the belly slide. With side-to-side twists of the body, the animal uses its legs to push along on its belly. This tobogganing movement is useful for fast escapes but is also used to slip quietly into the water.

▲ BEST FOOT FORWARD
The tracks of a saltwater crocodile in the mud show how its legs move in sequence. The right front leg goes forward first, then the back left leg. The front left leg goes forward next, and finally the right back leg moves. If the legs on the same side moved one after the other, the crocodile would overbalance.

▼ THE HIGH WALK
To move on land, crocodilians hold their legs underneath the body, lifting most of the tail off the ground. This is called the high walk. It is very different from the walk of a lizard, which keeps its legs sprawled out at the sides of its body. The tail is dragged behind the body in the high walk, but if the animal starts to run, the tail swings from side to side. A special ankle joint lets crocodilians twist and turn their legs in the high walk.

▲ FLOATING AROUND

This Nile crocodile is floating near the surface of Lake Tanganyika, Tanzania, Africa. It is holding its feet out to the sides for balance. The toes and the webbing between them are spread out for extra stability. In the water, the crocodile floats with its tail down, but as it moves its body becomes horizontal.

► TAIL WALKING

Some crocodilians can leap straight up out of the water. They seem to be walking on their tails in the same way that a dolphin can travel backward on its strong tail. This movement is, however, unusual. Large crocodiles will also spring upward, propelled by their back legs, to grab prey unawares.

► FEET AND TOES

On the front feet, crocodilians have five separate digits (toes). These sometimes have webbing (skin) stretched between them. The back feet are always webbed to help them balance and move in the water. There are only four toes on the back feet. The fifth toe is just a small bone inside the foot.

▲ THE GALLOP

The fastest way for a crocodilian to move on land is to gallop. Only a few crocodiles, such as the Johnston's crocodile shown above, make a habit of moving like this. In a gallop, the back legs push the crocodilian forward in a leap, and the front legs stretch out to catch the body as it lands at the end of the leap. Then the back legs swing forward to push the animal forward again.

Temperature Check

Soon after the sun rises, the first alligators heave themselves out of the river and flop down on the bank. The banks fill up quickly as more alligators join the first, warming their scaly bodies in the sun's rays. As the hours go by and the day becomes hotter, the alligators open their toothy jaws wide to cool down. Later in the day, they may go for a swim or crawl into the shade to cool off. As the air chills at night, the alligators slip back into the water again. This is because water stays warmer for longer at night than the land.

Crocodilians are cold-blooded, which means their body temperature varies with outside temperatures. To warm up or cool down, they move to warm or cool places. Their ideal body temperature is between 85 and 95°F.

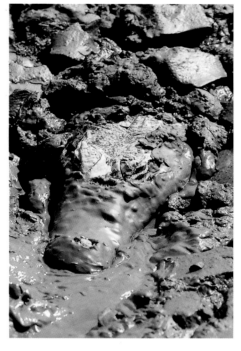

▲ **MUD PACK**
A spectacled caiman is buried deep in the mud to keep cool during the hot, dry season. Mud is like water and does not get as hot or as cold as dry land. It also helps to keep the caiman's scaly skin free from parasites and biting insects.

◄ **SOLAR PANELS**
The crested scutes on the tail of a crocodilian are like the bony plates on armored dinosaurs. They act like solar panels, picking up heat when the animal basks in the sun. They also open to let as much heat as possible escape from the body to cool down the body.

◄ UNDER THE ICE

An alligator can survive under a layer of ice as long as it keeps a breathing hole open. Only alligators stay active at temperatures as low as 53 or 59°F. They do not eat, however, because the temperature is too low for their digestive systems to work.

▼ OPEN WIDE

While a Nile crocodile suns itself on a rock it also opens its mouth in a wide gape. Gaping helps to prevent the crocodile from becoming too hot. The breeze flowing over the wide, wet surfaces of the mouth and tongue dries the moisture and, in turn, cools the blood. If you lick your finger and blow on it softly, you will notice that it feels a lot cooler.

▲ ALLIGATOR DAYS

Alligators follow a distinct daily routine when the weather is good, moving in and out of the water at regular intervals. They also enter the water if they are disturbed. In winter, alligators retreat into dens and become sleepy because their blood cools and slows them down.

► MEAL BREAKS

Being cold-blooded is quite useful in some ways. These alligators can bask in the sun without having to eat very much or very often. Warm-blooded animals such as mammals have to eat regularly. They need to eat about five times as much food as reptiles to keep their bodies warm.

Crocodilian Senses

The senses of sight, sound, smell, taste and touch are much more powerful in a crocodilian than in other living reptiles. They have good eyesight and can see in color. Their eyes are also adapted to seeing well in the dark, which is useful because they hunt mainly at night. Crocodilians also have acute hearing. They sense the sounds of danger or prey moving nearby and listen for the barks, coughs and roars of their own species at mating time. Crocodilians also have sensitive scales along the sides of their jaws, which help them to feel and capture prey.

▲ **NOISY GATOR**
An American alligator bellows loudly during courtship. Noises such as hissing or snarling are made at enemies. Young alligators call for help from adults. Small ear slits behind the eyes are kept open when the animal is out of the water. Flaps close to protect the ears when the animal submerges.

Did you know? Crocodiles shake their ear flaps up and down when they are angry.

▲ **SMELL DETECTORS**
A Nile crocodile picks up chemical signals through the nostrils at the tip of its snout. These messages help it detect prey and others of its kind. Crocodiles can smell food over long distances. They are known to have come from as far away as 2 mi. to feed together on the carcass of a large animal.

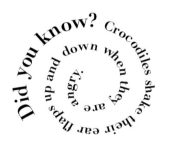

Crocodile Tears
According to legend, crocodiles cry to make people feel so sorry for them that they come near enough for the crocodiles to catch them. Crocodiles are also supposed to shed tears of remorse before finishing a meal. It is said that people cry crocodile tears when they seem to be sorry for something but really are not. Real-life crocodiles cannot cry but sometimes look as if they are.

► TASTY TONGUE

Inside the gaping mouth of an American crocodile is a wide, fleshy tongue. It is joined to the bottom of the mouth and does not move, so it plays no part in catching prey. We know that crocodilians have taste buds lining their mouths because some prefer one type of food to another. They can tell the difference between sweet and sour tastes. They also have salt glands on their tongues that get rid of excess salt. Salt builds up in the body over time if the animal lives in the sea or a very dry environment.

◄ GLOW-IN-THE-DARK EYES

A flashlight shone into a crocodile farm at night makes the dark glow eerily with a thousand living lights. The scientific explanation is that a special layer at the back of the eye reflects light back into the front of the eye. This ensures that the eye catches as much light as possible. Above water, crocodilians see well and are able to spot prey up to 295 ft away. Underwater, an inner, transparent lid covers the eye, making vision foggy, like looking through thick goggles.

► A PREDATOR'S EYE

The eye of a spectacled caiman, like all crocodilians, has both upper and lower lids. A third eyelid at the side, called a nictitating (blinking) membrane, moves across to clean the eye's surface. The dark, vertical pupil narrows to a slit to stop bright light from damaging the eye. At night, the pupil opens wide to let any available light into the eye. A round pupil, such as a human's, cannot open as wide.

Food and Hunting

How would it feel to wait up to two years for a meal? Amazingly, a big crocodile can probably survive this long between meals. It lives off fat stored in its tail and other parts of its body. Crocodilians eat a lot of fish, but their strong jaws will snap up anything that wanders too close, from birds, snakes and turtles to raccoons, zebras, cattle and horses. They also eat dead animals. Young crocodilians eat small animals such as insects, snails and frogs.

Most crocodilians sit and wait for their food to come to them, which saves energy. They also catch their meals by stalking and surprising prey. The three main ways of capturing and killing food are lunging toward prey, leaping up out of the water and sweeping their jaws open from side to side through the water. Most crocodilians hunt at night. They eat every part of their prey, including the bones.

▲ SURPRISE ATTACK
A Nile crocodile lunges from the water at an incredible speed to grab a wildebeest in its powerful jaws. It is difficult for the wildebeest to jump back, as the riverbank slopes steeply into the water. The crocodile will plunge back into the water, dragging its prey with it in order to drown it.

▼ BOLD BIRDS
Large crocodiles feed on big wading birds such as this saddlebill stork. Birds, however, often seem to know when they are in no danger from a crocodile. Plovers have been seen standing on the gums of crocodiles and even pecking at their teeth for leftovers. A marabou stork was once seen stealing a fish right out of a crocodile's mouth.

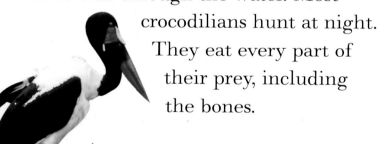

► SMALLER PREY

A dwarf caiman lies in wait to snap up a tasty bullfrog. Small species of crocodilian like this caiman, as well as young crocodilians, eat a lot of frogs and toads. Youngsters also snap up beetles, spiders, giant water bugs and small fishes. They will leap into the air to catch dragonflies and other insects hovering over the water. Small crocodilians are also preyed upon by their larger relatives.

crocodilians have varied diets and will eat any animal they can catch

◄ SWALLOWING PREY

A crocodile raises its head and grips a crab firmly at the back of its throat. After several jerky head movements the crab is correctly positioned to be eaten whole. High levels of acid in the crocodile's stomach help it break down the crab's hard shell so that every part is digested.

Did you know? A Nile crocodile has a stomach that is about the size of a basketball.

► FISHY FOOD

A Nile crocodile swallows a fish head first. This stops any spines it has from sticking in the crocodile's throat. About 70 percent of the diet of most crocodilians is fish. Crocodilians with narrow snouts, such as the gharial, Johnston's crocodile and the African slender-snouted crocodile, feed mainly on fish. Fish are caught with a sideways, snapping movement that is easier and faster with a slender snout.

Focus on a

1 A Nile crocodile is nearly invisible, as it lies almost submerged in wait for its prey. Only its eyes, ears and nostrils are showing. It lurks in places where it knows prey regularly visit the river. Its dark olive color provides effective camouflage. To disappear completely it can vanish beneath the water. Some crocodilians can hold their breath for more than an hour while submerged.

A crocodile quietly drifting near the shore looks just like a harmless, floating log. This is just a disguise as it waits for an unsuspecting animal to come down to the river to drink. The crocodile is in luck. A herd of zebras come to cross the river. The crocodile launches its attack with astonishing speed. Shooting forward, it snaps shut its powerful jaws and sharp teeth like a vice around a zebra's leg or muzzle. The stunned zebra is pulled into deeper water to be drowned. Other crocodiles are attracted to the large kill. They gather around to bite into the carcass, rotating in the water to twist off large chunks of flesh. Grazing animals constantly risk death-by-crocodile to drink or cross water. There is little they can do to defend themselves from the attack of such a large predator.

2 The crocodile erupts from the water, taking the zebras by surprise. It lunges at its victim with a quick burst of energy. It is important for the crocodile to overcome its prey quickly, as it cannot chase it overland. The crocodile is also easily exhausted and takes a long time to recover from exercise of any kind.

Crocodile's Lunch

3 The crocodile seizes, pulls and shakes the zebra in its powerful jaws. Sometimes the victim's neck is broken in the attack, and it dies quickly. More often the shocked animal is dragged into the water, struggling feebly against its attacker.

4 The crocodile drags the zebra into deeper water and holds it down to drown it. It may also spin around, until the prey stops breathing. The crocodile continues to spin around with the prey clamped in its jaws, until it is dead.

5 A freshly killed zebra attracts Nile crocodiles from all around. A large kill is too difficult for one crocodile to defend on its own. Several crocodiles take turns sharing the feast and may help each other tear the carcass apart. They fasten their jaws onto a leg or lump of muscle and twist it in the water like a rotating shaft, until a chunk of meat is torn loose and can be swallowed.

Communication

Crocodilians pass on messages to each other by means of sounds, body language, smells and touch. Unlike other reptiles, they have a remarkable social life. Groups gather together for basking, sharing food, courting and nesting. Communication begins in the egg and continues throughout life. Adults are particularly sensitive to hatchling and juvenile distress calls and respond with threats or actual attacks. Sounds are made with the vocal cords and with other parts of the body, such as slapping the head against the surface of the water. Crocodilians also use visual communication. Body postures and special movements show which individuals are strong and dominant. Weaker individuals signal to show that they recognize a dominant individual to avoid fighting and injury.

▲ **HEAD BANGER**
A crocodile lifts its head out of the water, jaws open. The jaws slam shut just before they smack the surface of the water. This is called the head slap and makes a loud pop followed by a splash. Head slapping may be a sign of dominance and is often used during the breeding season.

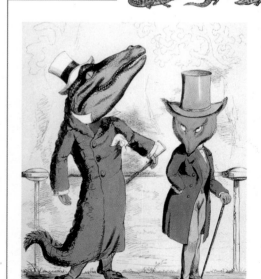

The Fox and the Crocodile
In this Aesop's fable, the fox and the crocodile meet one day. The crocodile boasts at length about its cunning as a hunter. Then the fox says, "That's all very impressive, but tell me, what am I wearing on my feet?" The crocodile looks down and there, on the fox's feet, is a pair of shoes made from crocodile skin.

▲ **GHARIAL MESSAGES**
The gharial does not head slap, but claps its jaws underwater during the breeding season. Sound travels faster through water than air, so sound signals are very useful for aquatic life.

▶ INFRASOUNDS

Some crocodilians make sounds by rapidly squeezing their torso muscles just beneath the surface of the water. The water bubbles up and bounces off the back. The sounds produced are at a very low level, so we can hardly hear them. At close range, they sound like distant thunder. These infrasounds travel quickly over long distances through the water and may be part of courtship. Sometimes they are produced before bellowing, roaring or head slaps.

Did you know? The bellow of an alligator can be heard at least 490 ft away.

◀ I AM THE GREATEST

Dominant animals are usually bigger and more aggressive than submissive ones. They show off their importance by swimming boldly at the surface or thrashing their tails from side to side on land. Weaker individuals usually only lift their heads out of the water and expose their vulnerable throats. This shows that they submit and do not want to fight.

▶ GETTING TOGETHER

These caimans are gathering together at the start of the rainy season in Brazil. Crocodilians often come together in loose groups—for example, when they are basking, nesting or sharing food. They tend to ignore each other once dominance battles have been established. During a long, dry spell, large numbers of crocodilians often gather together at water holes to share the remaining water. Young crocodilians stay in a close group for the first months of life as there is safety in numbers.

Choosing a Mate

Male and female crocodilians are often difficult to tell apart. Only male gharials are immediately recognizable, distinguished from females by the bumps on the ends of their snouts. Most males are larger, and grow and mature more quickly than females. They are ready to mate at about seven years old; females are ready at about nine.

In some species, groups of adults gather in the breeding season and set up special mating territories. In other species, mating takes place in long-established territories. Females often begin the courtship process. Courtship behavior includes bellowing and grunting, rubbing heads and bodies, blowing bubbles, circling and riding on the partner's back.

▲ BUMPY NOSE

Most male gharials have a strange bump, or pot, on the end of the snout near their nostrils. Females have flat snouts. No one is quite sure what the bump is for, but it is probably used in courtship. It may help the male to change hissing sounds into buzzing sounds, as air vibrates inside the hollow bump.

◄ COURTING COUPLE

Crocodilians touch each other a lot during courtship, especially around the head and neck. Males will also try to impress females by bubbling water from the nostrils and mouth. An interested female arches her back, then raises her head with her mouth open. The two may push each other underwater to see how big and strong their partner is.

32

◄ SWEET-SMELLING SCENT

Crocodilians have little bumps under their lower jaws. These are musk glands. The musk is a sweet-smelling, greenish, oily perfume. It produces a scent that attracts the opposite sex. Musk glands are more noticeable in males. During courtship, the male may rub his throat across the female's head and neck. This releases the scent from the musk glands and helps to prepare the female for mating.

► FIGHTING MALES

Male crocodilians may fight each other for the chance to court and mate with females. They may spar with their jaws open or make themselves look bigger and more powerful by puffing up their bodies with air. Saltwater crocodiles are particularly violent and bash their heads together with a loud thud. These contests may go on for an hour or more but do not seem to cause much permanent damage.

◄ THE MATING GAME

Courtship can last for up to two hours before mating occurs. The couple sinks underwater, and the male wraps his tail around his partner. Mating takes only a few minutes. The couple mates several times during the day. A dominant male may mate with up to 20 females in the breeding season. Females, too, mate with other males, although the dominant male tries to prevent this.

33

Focus on

1 Male and female alligators do not live together all year round. They come together in spring to court and mate. The rest of the year they glide through the swamp, searching for food or basking in the sun. In winter they rest in cozy dens.

Early in April or May, American alligators begin courtship rituals. Males fight each other to win their own territories. The biggest and strongest males win the best territories. Their musk glands give off a strong, sweet smell, attractive to females. Female alligators do not have territories. They visit the territories of several males and may mate several times. Once a female and a male have mated, they part. The female builds a nest in June or July and lays her eggs. In about 60 to 70 days, the young alligators begin to hatch and the female digs them out of the nest and carries them to water. She remains with her young for months or even years.

2 The American alligator is the noisiest crocodilian. Males and females make bellowing noises especially in the breeding season. Males bellow loudly to warn other males to keep out of their territories and to let females know where they are. Each alligator has a different voice, which sounds like the throaty roar of a stalling motorboat engine. The sound carries for long distances in the swamp. Once one alligator starts to bellow, others soon join in and may continue for half an hour.

Alligators

3 In the mating season bulls (males) test each other to see who is the biggest and strongest. They push and wrestle and sometimes fight violently. The strongest males win the best territories for food and water. Bellowing helps to limit serious fighting. Other males stay away from areas where they have heard a loud bull.

4 Alligators mate in shallow water. Before mating, there is a slow courtship consisting of slapping the water and rubbing each other's muzzle and neck. Mating usually lasts only a minute or two before the pair separates. Alligators may mate with several partners in a season.

5 The female alligator uses her body, legs and tail to build a nest out of sand, soil and plants. It takes about two weeks to build and may be up to 30 in high and 6 ft across. In the middle the female digs a hole and lines it with mud. She lays between 20 and 70 eggs, which she then covers up. She stays near the nest site while the eggs develop, guarding them from raccoons and other predators.

Building a Nest

About a month after mating, a female crocodilian is ready to lay her eggs on land. First she builds a nest to keep her eggs warm. If the temperature stays below 82°F, the babies will die before they hatch. The temperature inside the nest determines whether the hatchlings are male or female. Females build their nests at night. Alligators, caimans and some crocodiles build nests that are solid mounds of fresh plants and soil. Other crocodiles, and gharials, dig holes in the sand with their back feet. Some species dig trial nests before they dig the real one. This may be to check that the temperature is right for the eggs to develop. Nest sites are chosen to be near water but above the floodwater mark. The females often stay close to the nest to guard it against predators, even while searching for food.

▲ **SHARING NESTS**
Turtles, such as this red-bellied turtle, sometimes lay their eggs in crocodilian nests to save them the hard work of making their own nests. The eggs are protected by the fierce crocodilian mother, who guards her own eggs and the turtle's eggs. As many as 200 red-bellied turtle eggs have been found in alligator nests.

◄ **NEST MOUNDS**
A Morelet's crocodile has raked soil and uprooted plant material into a big pile to build her nest mound. She uses her body to press it all together firmly. Then she scoops out a hole in the mound with her back feet. She lays her eggs in the hole and then closes the top of the nest. As the plant material rots, it gives off heat, which keeps the eggs warm.

Did you know? Male crocodilians do not help make nests.

▼ IS IT A BOY OR A GIRL?

A saltwater crocodile, like all crocodilians, keeps its eggs at about 86 to 89°F inside the nest. The temperatures during the first few weeks after the eggs are laid is crucial. This controls whether the babies are male or female. Higher temperatures, such as 89 to 91°F, produce more males, while temperatures of 88°F or lower produce more females. Temperature also affects the color and body patterns of the babies.

▲ A SANDY NEST

Nile crocodiles dig their nests on sandy riverbanks, beaches or lakesides. Females may compete for nest sites by trying to push each other over. Larger, heavier females usually win these contests. The female uses her back legs for digging, so the nest burrow is dug to a depth of about the same length as her back legs.

► NESTING TOGETHER

Female Nile crocodiles often nest together. A female may even return to the same breeding ground and nest site each year. Each female guards her nest, either by lying right on top of the nest or watching it from the nearby shade.

◄ NEST THIEF

The monitor lizard often digs its way into crocodile nests in Africa and Asia to eat the eggs. In Africa, these lizards may sometimes steal over half of all the eggs laid.

Developing Eggs

All crocodilians lay white, oval eggs with hard shells like those of a bird. The number of eggs laid by one female at a time varies from about 10 to 90, depending on the species and the age of the mother. Older females lay more eggs. The length of time it takes for the eggs to hatch varies with the species and the temperature, but takes from 55 to 110 days. During this time, called the incubation period, the weather can affect the babies developing inside the eggs. Too much rain can drown the babies before they are born as water can seep through the shells. Hot weather may cause the inside of the egg to overheat. This hardens the yolk so that the baby cannot absorb it and starves to death. Another danger is that eggs laid by one female are accidentally dug up and destroyed by another female digging a nest in the same place.

▲ HANDFUL OF EGGS
In many countries, people eat crocodilian eggs. They harvest them from nests for sale at the local market. This person is holding the eggs of a gharial. Each egg weighs about 3 oz. The mother gharial lays about 40 eggs in a hole in the sand. She lays them in two tiers, separated from each other by a fairly thick layer of sand, and may spend several hours covering her nest.

► LAYING EGGS
The mugger, or swamp, crocodile of India digs a sandy pit about 20 in. deep in a river bank and lays 10 to 50 eggs inside. She lays her eggs in layers and then covers them with a mound of twigs, leaves, soil and sand. During the 50- to 75-day incubation, the female spends most of the time practically on top of the nest. When females lay their eggs, they are usually quite tame. Researchers have been able to catch the eggs as they are laid.

► INSIDE AN EGG

Curled tightly inside its egg, this alligator has its head and tail twisted around its belly. Next to the developing baby is a supply of yolk, which provides it with food during incubation. Researchers have removed the top third of the shell to study the stages of development. The baby will develop normally even though some of the shell is missing. As the eggs develop, they give off carbon dioxide gas into the nest. This reacts with air in the chamber and may make the shell thinner to let in more oxygen.

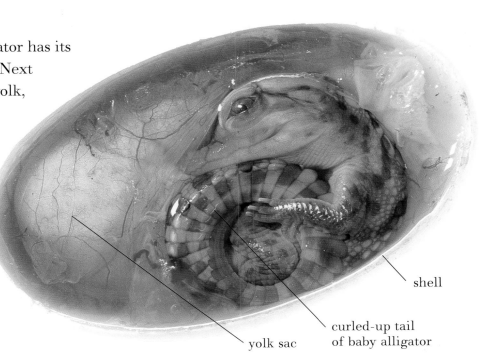

shell

curled-up tail
of baby alligator

yolk sac

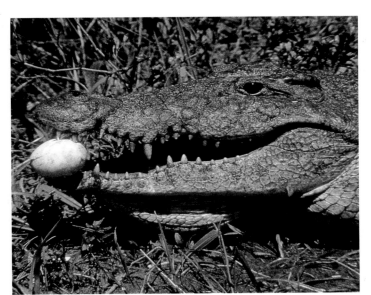

◄ CRACKING EGGS

Mother crocodiles sometimes help eggs to hatch. When she hears the baby calling inside, she picks up the egg in her mouth. Holding it gently, she rolls the egg back and forth against the roof of her mouth, pressing gently to crack the shell. The mother may have to do this for about 20 minutes before the baby breaks free from the egg.

Did you know? A large crocodile may take an hour to lay 80 or more eggs.

► EGGS IN THE NEST

Saltwater crocodiles lay large, creamy-white eggs, up to twice the size of chicken's eggs. However, the eggs are more equally rounded at each end than chicken's eggs. It takes a female saltwater crocodile about 15 minutes to lay between 20 and 90 eggs in her nest. The eggs take up to 90 days to hatch.

Focus on

Baby crocodilians make yelping, croaking and grunting noises from inside their eggs when it is time to hatch. The mother hears the noises and digs the eggs from the nest. The babies struggle free of their eggshells, sometimes with help from their mother. While the young are hatching, the mother is in a very aggressive mood and will attack any animal that comes near. The hatchlings are about 11 inches long, lively and very agile. They can give a human finger a painful nip with their sharp teeth. Their mother carries them gently in her mouth down to the water. She opens her jaws and gently twists her head from side to side to wash the babies out of her mouth.

1 As soon as a mother Nile crocodile hears her babies calling from inside their eggs, she knows it is time to help them escape from the nest. She scrapes off the soil and sand with her front feet and may even use her teeth to cut through any roots that have grown between the eggs. Her help is very important, as the soil has hardened during incubation. The hatchlings would find it difficult to dig their way up to the surface without her help.

the hatchling punches a hole in its hard shell with a forward-pointing egg tooth

2 This baby Nile crocodile has just broken through its eggshell. It used a horny tip on the snout, called the egg tooth to break through. The egg tooth is the size of a grain of sand and disappears after about a week. The egg has become thinner during the long incubation. This makes it easier for the baby to break free.

Hatching

3 Struggling out of an egg is a long, exhausting process for the hatchling. When the babies are half out of their eggs, they sometimes take a break so they can rest before completely leaving their shells. After hatching, the mother crushes or swallows rotten eggs.

4 Even though they are fierce predators, crocodilians make caring parents. The mother Nile crocodile lowers her head into the nest and delicately picks up the hatchlings, as well as any unhatched eggs, between her sharp teeth. She puts them into her mouth. The weight of all the babies and eggs pushes down on her tongue to form a pouch that holds up to 20 eggs and live young. Male mugger crocodiles also carry the young like this and help hatchlings to escape from their eggs.

5 A young crocodilian's belly looks fat when it hatches. This is because it contains the remains of the yolk sac, which nourished it through the incubation period. The hatchling can swim and catch its own food right away, but it continues to feed on the yolk sac for up to two weeks. In Africa, the wet season usually starts soon after baby Nile crocodiles hatch. This provides an abundance of food, such as insects, tadpoles, and frogs, for the hatchlings. They are very vulnerable to predators and are guarded by their mother for a least the first weeks of life.

Growing Up

Juvenile (young) crocodilians lead a very dangerous life. They are too small to defend themselves easily, despite their sharp teeth. Their bright colors also make them easy for predators to spot. All sorts of predators lurk in the water and on the shore, from birds of prey and monitor lizards to otters, pelicans, tiger fish and even other crocodilians. One of the reasons that crocodilians lay so many eggs is that so many young do not survive to reach their first birthday. Only one in ten alligators lives to the end of its first year. Juveniles often stay together in groups during the first weeks of life and call loudly to the adults for help if they are in danger. By the time the juveniles are four years old, they stop making distress calls and start responding to the calls of other young individuals.

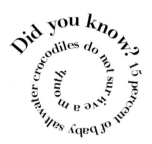

▲ INSECT DIET
A spiky-jawed Johnston's crocodile is about to snap up a damselfly. Juveniles eat mainly insects. As they grow, they take larger prey, such as snails, shrimps, crabs and small fish. Their snouts gradually strengthen, so that they are able to catch bigger prey. At a few months old, they live much like lizards and move quite a distance away from the water.

Did you know? 15 percent of baby saltwater crocodiles do not survive a month.

◄ FAST FOOD
These juvenile alligators will grow twice as fast in captivity as they would in the wild. This is because they are fed regular meals and do not have to wait until they can catch a meal for themselves. It is also because they are kept in warm water—alligators stop feeding in cooler water. The best temperature for growth is 86 to 90°F.

▶ BABY CARRIERS

Juveniles stay close to their mother for the first few weeks, often using her back to rest on. No predator would dare to attack them there. Baby alligators are only about 10 in. long when they are born but they grow very quickly. When they have enough food to eat, male alligators grow about 12 in. a year until they are 15 years of age.

▲ CROC AND POD

A Nile crocodile guards her young while they bask in the sun. A group of crocodilian young is called a pod. A pod may stay in the same area for as long as two years. At the first sign of danger, the mother rapidly vibrates her trunk muscles, and the young immediately dive underwater.

▲ TOO MANY ENEMIES

The list of land predators that attack juvenile crocodilians include big cats such as this leopard, ground hornbills, marabou storks and genet cats. Large wading birds, including herons, spear them with their sharp beaks in shallow water while, in deeper water, catfish, otters and turtles all enjoy a young crocodilian as a snack. Only about two percent of all the eggs laid each year survive to hatch and grow into adults.

▶ NOISY POD

A pod of juveniles, like this group of young caimans, is a noisy bunch. By chirping and yelping for help, a juvenile warns its brothers and sisters that there is a predator nearby. The siblings quickly dive for shelter and hope that an adult will come to protect them. If a young Nile crocodile strays from its pod, it makes loud distress calls. Its mother, or any other female nearby, will pick up the youngster in her jaws and carry it back to the group.

On the Defensive

By the time a crocodilian has grown to about 3 feet long, very few predators will threaten it. The main dangers to adult crocodilians come from large animals, such as jaguars, lions, elephants and hippopotamuses, who attack to protect their young. Giant snakes called anacondas will attack and kill crocodilians for food. Adults may also be killed during battles with other crocodilians during the breeding season. People are the main enemy of crocodilians. They kill them for their skins, for food or when they become dangerous. Crocodilians are protected by their powerful jaws, strong tail and heavy armor. They can also swim away from danger and hide underwater, in the mud or among plants.

▲ KEEP AWAY!

An American alligator puffs up its body with air to look bigger and more threatening. It lets out the air quickly to make a hissing sound. If an enemy is still not scared away, the alligator will then attack.

► THE HIDDEN EYE

What sort of animal is peeping out from underneath a green carpet of floating water plants? It is hard to tell that there is a saltwater crocodile lurking just beneath the surface. Crocodilians feel safer in the water because they are such good swimmers. They may spend hours almost completely underwater, keeping very still, waiting for prey to come by or for danger to pass. They move so quietly and smoothly that the vegetation on top of the water is hardly disturbed.

▶ CAMOUFLAGE COLORS

The color of crocodilians blends in well with their surroundings. Many species change color all the time. For example, at warmer times of the day, they may become lighter in color. During cool parts of the day, such as the morning, they may look duller and are often mistaken for logs.

◀ CAIMAN FOR LUNCH

A deadly anaconda squeezes the life out of an unfortunate caiman. The anaconda of South America lives partly in the water and can grow up to 30 ft long. It can easily kill a caiman by twisting its strong coils around the caiman's body until the victim cannot breathe any more. The caiman dies slowly, either from suffocation or shock. However, anacondas only kill caimans occasionally—they are not an important part of the snake's diet.

Ticking Croc

One of the most famous crocodiles in literature is in Peter Pan, *written by J. M. Barrie in 1904. Peter Pan's greatest enemy is Captain Hook. In a fair fight, Peter cuts off Hook's left hand, which is eaten by a crocodile. The crocodile follows Hook's ship, hoping for a chance to gobble up the rest of him. He makes a ticking noise as he travels because he swallowed a clock. At the end, Hook falls into the water. He is chased by the crocodile, but we do not find out if he eats him.*

▲ HUMAN DANGERS

People have always killed small numbers of crocodilians for food, as this Brazilian family has done. However, the shooting of crocodilians through fear or for sport has had a much more severe impact on their population. Of the 22 species of crocodilian, 17 have been hunted to the verge of extinction.

45

Freshwater Habitats

A habitat is a place where an animal lives. Most crocodilians live in freshwater habitats, such as rivers, lakes, marshes and swamps, and in warm places. They tend to live in shallow areas because they need to be able to crawl onto dry land for basking and laying their eggs. The shallow water also has many plants to hide among and plenty of animals to eat. The temperature of the water does not vary as much as temperatures on dry land do. This helps a crocodilian keep its body temperature steady. Crocodilians save energy by moving around in water rather than on dry land because the water supports their heavy bodies. Crocodilians also make an impact on their habitats. The American alligator, for example, digs holes in the river bed. These are cool places where alligators and other animals hide during the heat of the day.

▲ **GATOR HOLES**
American alligators living in the Florida Everglades dig large gator holes in the limestone river bed. In the dry season, these holes stay full of water. They provide a vital water supply that keeps the alligators and many other animals alive.

▲ **RIVER DWELLERS**
The gharial likes fast-flowing rivers with high banks, clear water and deep pools where there are plenty of fish. It inhabits rivers such as the Indus in Pakistan, the Ganges in India and the Brahmaputra of Bangladesh and Assam.

Aboriginal Creation Myth
Crocodiles are often shown in bark paintings and rock art made by the Aboriginals of Australia. Their creation myth, called the "dream time," tells how ancestral animals created the land and people. According to a

Gunwinggu story from Arnhem Land, the Liverpool River was made by a crocodile ancestor. The mighty crocodile made his way from the mountains to the sea, chewing the land as he went. This made deep furrows, which filled with water to become the river.

◄ SEASONAL CHANGE

During the dry season, caimans gather in the few remaining pools along a drying-up river bed. Although the pools become very crowded, the caimans seem to get along well together. In some parts of South America, caimans are forced to live in river pools for four or five months of the year. After the floods of the wet season, they can spread out again.

► NILE CROCODILES

Nile crocodiles warm themselves in the sun on a sandy riverbank. Despite their name, Nile crocodiles do not live only in the river Nile. At one time, these powerful crocodiles lived all over Africa, except in the desert areas. Nowadays, they still live in parts of the Nile, as well as the other African waterways such as the Limpopo and Senegal rivers, Lake Chad and the Okavango swamp. There are also Nile crocodiles living on the island of Madagascar.

◄ AUSTRALIAN HABITATS

Australian crocodiles, such as Johnston's crocodile, often live in billabongs (waterholes), such as this one in the Northern Territory of Australia. They provide crocodiles with water and land as well as food to eat. A billabong is a branch of a river that comes to a dead end. Saltwater crocodiles are also found in such areas because they live in both fresh and salt water. People are advised not to swim or wade in the water and to avoid camping nearby.

Rainforest Dwellers

Three unusual crocodilians live in rainforest streams and swamps where they avoid competition with larger caimans and crocodiles. Cuvier's dwarf caiman and Schneider's dwarf caiman live in South America, while the African dwarf crocodile lives in the tropical forests of Central Africa. The bodies of these small crocodilians are heavily armored. This may help to protect the South American caimans from sharp rocks in the fast-flowing streams where they live and from spiky plants in the forest. All three crocodilians may also need this extra protection from predators because of their small size. Rainforest crocodilians do not usually bask in the sun during the day, although the dwarf crocodile may sometimes climb trees to sun itself. All three crocodilians seem to spend quite a lot of time on land. Schneider's dwarf caiman lives in burrows dug in stream banks.

▲ MYSTERIOUS CROC

Very little is known about the African dwarf crocodile. It is a secretive and shy animal that is active at night. It lives in swamps, ponds and small, slow-moving streams. After heavy rain, the dwarf crocodile may make long trips over land at night. Females lay about ten eggs, which take 100 days to hatch. They probably protect their young in their first weeks.

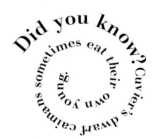

Did you know? Cuvier's dwarf caimans sometimes eat their own young.

◄ YOUNG COLORS

A newly hatched Cuvier's dwarf caiman rests on a rock. Hatchling dwarf caimans have a yellowish-brown skull and black or brown crossbands on the body and tail. This is helpful for camouflage. For the first couple of days, they are also covered in slime. Then they enter the water for the first time.

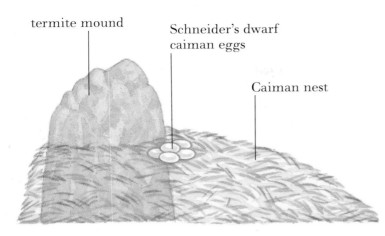

termite mound

Schneider's dwarf caiman eggs

Caiman nest

termite mound

edge of nest

82°F

83°F

84°F

86°F

90°F

93°F

3 feet

◀ HELPFUL NEIGHBORS

Schneider's dwarf caiman lays its eggs beside termite mounds. Little sun reaches the forest floor, so the extra heat generated by the termites helps the caiman's eggs develop. Often, the termites cover the eggs with a rock-hard layer, so the parents must help their young break out.

▲ NOSE TO TAIL

Unlike other caimans, dwarf caimans do not have bony ridges around the eyes and snout. Because of this they are also known as smooth-fronted caimans. Shown here is Cuvier's dwarf caiman. Its short snout is not streamlined for swimming, and it has a short tail, which may help it to move more easily on land.

◀ TEETH AND DIET

The sharp, pointed teeth of Cuvier's dwarf caiman curve backward in the mouth. This helps it grip the slippery skin of frogs or seize such prey as fish in fast-flowing waters. The Cuvier's diet is not well known, but it probably eats a variety of aquatic invertebrates (animals without a backbone), such as shrimps and crabs, as well as rodents, birds and snakes.

MARKINGS FOR LIFE
A black caiman hatches from its egg. Its mother laid up to 65 eggs in the nest, which hatched six weeks later. Its strong markings stay as it grows.

THE SPECTACLED CAIMAN
The spectacled caiman is so called because of the bony ridges around its eye sockets and across the top of the muzzle. These look a bit like eye glasses and may help to strengthen its skull as it seizes and kills prey.

BIG HEAD
The broad-snouted caiman has the widest head of any crocodilian, with a ridge running down the snout. It is about 6 ft long and lives in marshes or small streams with dense vegetation.

Focus on

Caimans are mostly small, agile crocodilians that live in Central or South America. Most do not grow more than 7 feet long, but the black caiman can be bigger than an alligator (their closest relative). Caimans look like alligators because their lower teeth do not show when their mouths are closed. They have sharper, longer teeth than alligators and strong, bony plates on the belly and back, including eight bony scutes on the back of the neck. This bony armor helps to protect them from predators, even humans (as tough skin is unsuitable for leather goods). Many caimans are endangered, but some spectacled caimans are very adaptable. They have taken over habitats where American crocodiles and black caimans have been hunted to extinction.

Caimans

young caimans have spots
and bands across the body

black caiman
(*Melanosuchus niger*)

bony scutes

unusual webbed front feet

short, low snout
with jaws lined
with 64 teeth

TYPICAL CAIMAN

Caimans have short snouts, roughly
circular eye sockets and wrinkled
eyelids. Although caimans are
closely related to alligators,
they are quicker and move
more like crocodiles.

EGG THIEF

Tegu lizards eat caiman eggs. In
some areas, over 80 percent of the
nests are destroyed by these large
lizards. Female caimans may nest
together to help defend their eggs.

CAPABLE CAIMAN

The black caiman is the largest of all caimans.
The one shown here has just
snapped up a piranha. Black
caimans can grow to over 19 ft long
and have sharp eyesight and hearing.
They hunt for capybaras (South
American rodents) and fish after dusk.
When black caimans disappear, the balance
of life in an area is upset. Hunted for killing
cattle, they are now an endangered species.

Saltwater Species

Most crocodilians live in fresh water, but a few venture into estuaries (the mouths of rivers), coastal swamps or the sea. American and Nile crocodiles and spectacled caimans have been found in saltwater habitats. The crocodilian most often seen at sea is the saltwater crocodile, also known as the Indopacific or estuarine crocodile. It is found in a vast area, from southern India to Fiji, and although usually found in rivers and lakes, it has been seen hundreds of miles from the nearest land. Hatchlings are even reared in seawater. This species has efficient salt glands on its tongue to get rid of extra salt without losing too much water. It is a mystery why freshwater crocodiles also have these glands, but it may be because their ancestors lived in the sea. Alligators and caimans do not have salt glands.

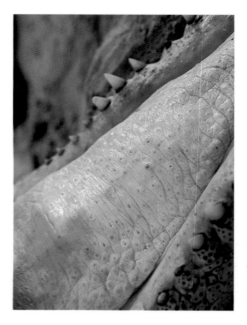

▲ SALTY TONGUE
Crocodiles have up to 40 salt glands on the tongue. These special salivary glands let the crocodile get rid of excess salt without losing too much water. These glands are necessary because crocodiles have kidneys that need plenty of water to flush out the salt. At sea there is too little fresh water for this to happen.

► SCALY DRIFTER
Although it can swim vast distances far out to sea, a saltwater crocodile is generally a lazy creature. Slow, side-to-side sweeps of a long, muscular tail propel the crocodile through the water, using as little energy as possible. Saltwater crocodiles do not like to have to swim vigorously, so they avoid strong waves wherever possible. They prefer to drift with the tide in relatively calm water.

► **NEW WORLD CROC**

The American crocodile is the most widespread crocodile in the Americas, ranging from southern Florida to the Pacific coast of Peru. It grows up to 19 ft in length (11 ft on average) and lives in mangrove swamps, estuaries and lagoons as well as fresh and brackish (slightly salty) coastal rivers. It has the least armor (bony scutes) of any crocodilian and a hump on the snout between the eyes and nostrils.

◄ **TRAVELING CAIMANS**

A group of baby spectacled, or common, caimans hides among the leaves of aquatic plants. This wide-ranging species lives in all sorts of habitats, including saltwater ones, such as salt marshes. They even live on islands, such as Trinidad and Tobago in the Caribbean.

◄ **LOST ARMOR**

A saltwater crocodile has less protective armor on the neck and back compared to other crocodilians. This makes it easier for the crocodile to bend its body when swimming. Thick, heavy scales would weigh it down too much at sea.

▲ **NILE CROCODILE**

Nile crocodiles typically live in rivers, but they also inhabit salty estuaries and mangrove swamps. Sometimes they are found on Kenyan beaches and may be swept out to sea. Some have reached the islands of Zanzibar and Madagascar.

53

Ancient Crocodiles

The first alligators and crocodiles lived at the same time as the dinosaurs. Some were even powerful enough to kill the biggest plant-eating dinosaurs. The crocodiles lived through whatever disaster wiped out the dinosaurs, probably because they can go for so long without food. The first crocodiles, the protosuchians, lived about 200 million years ago. They were small land animals with long legs and short snouts. From 200 to 65 million years ago, long-snouted mesosuchians lived mainly in the sea, while the dinosaurs dominated the land. The closest ancestors of today's crocodilians were the early eusuchians, which developed about 80 million years ago. They looked much like gharials, with long snouts, and probably lurked in the shallow fresh waters of rivers and swamps. Like today's crocodilians, the eusuchians could breathe through their nostrils even when their mouths were open underwater. This made it possible for them to catch their prey in the water.

▲ FIRST CROCODILE
The name of this ancient crocodile, *Protosuchus*, means "first crocodile." It lived about 200 million years ago in Arizona and looked much like a lizard. *Protosuchus* was small, probably no more than 3 ft long, with a small, flat skull and a short snout.

▼ BACK TO THE SEA
Swimming along the shores and estuaries in Jurassic times, from about 200 to 145 million years ago, the most widespread crocodilian was *Stenosaurus*. It looked like modern-day gharials, although it is not related to them. *Stenosaurus* had a flexible body and a powerful tail, which allowed it to swim after fast-moving prey.

long, slender snout and up to 200 piercing teeth for trapping fish

▶ DINOSAUR DAYS

Goniopholis, shown here, was more dependent on land than many of its fellow mesosuchians. It looked much like a broad-snouted crocodile of today. *Goniopholis* had two or more rows of armor on its back and well-developed armor on its belly as well. Most mesosuchians lived in the sea. They were long-snouted with many piercing teeth for catching fish.

◀ MONSTER CROCODILE

Lurking in rivers and lakes 70 million years ago was a gigantic crocodile called *Deinosuchus*, which grew perhaps 50 ft long. It was a similar size to *T. rex* and big enough to eat quite large dinosaurs, such as the duck-billed dinosaurs. It had strong teeth and legs, vertebrae (spine bones) that were each 12 in. long and heavy protective scales shielding the body and the tail.

▶ SURVIVORS

Crocodilians are survivors of a world inhabited by dinosaurs. However, the origins of both dinosaurs and crocodilians date back much further, to a group of animals called thecodontians, which lived some 200 million years ago.

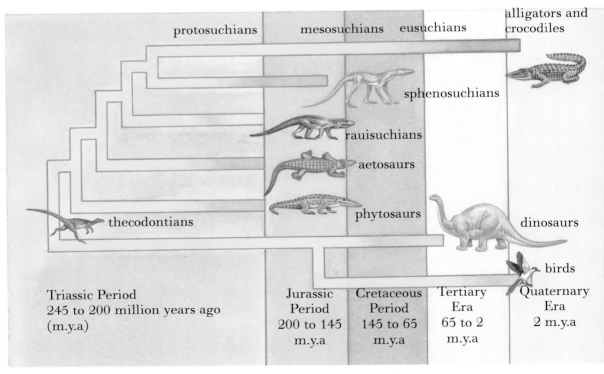

protosuchians   mesosuchians   eusuchians   alligators and crocodiles

sphenosuchians

rauisuchians

aetosaurs

thecodontians   phytosaurs   dinosaurs

birds

Triassic Period 245 to 200 million years ago (m.y.a)	Jurassic Period 200 to 145 m.y.a	Cretaceous Period 145 to 65 m.y.a	Tertiary Era 65 to 2 m.y.a	Quaternary Era 2 m.y.a

Living Relatives

Although it seems strange, birds are probably the closest living relatives of crocodilians. Crocodilians and birds have a long outer ear canal, a muscular gizzard to grind up food and a heart made up of four chambers. They both build nests and look after their young. The next closest living relatives of crocodilians are the group of reptiles called lepidosaurs, which includes the tuatara of New Zealand, lizards and snakes. The skin of lepidosaurs is usually covered by overlapping scales made of keratin (the substance fingernails are made of). Crocodilians and lepidosaurs both have two large openings on the cheek region of the skull, called a diapsid skull. Crocodilians are also more distantly related to the other main group of reptiles, turtles and tortoises.

▼ DINOSAUR SURVIVOR

The rare tuatara is found only on a few islands off the north coast of New Zealand. Here there are no rats or dogs to eat their eggs and hatchlings. They have hardly changed in appearance for millions of years and first appeared before dinosaurs lived on the earth.

▲ NESTING HABITS

The nests of some birds, such as this mallee fowl, are very similar to those of crocodilians. The mallee fowl builds a huge mound of wet leaves and twigs covered with wet sand. The female then lays her eggs in the middle of the mound.

▲ A SANDY NEST

Green turtles live in the sea, but lay their eggs on sandy beaches. The female drags herself up the beach and digs a hole in which to lay her eggs. Then she returns to the sea, leaving the baby turtles to fend for themselves when they eventually hatch.

American alligator
skull

eye socket

iguana skull

▶ DIAPSID SKULLS

Crocodilians, and lizards such as iguanas, both have two large openings on each side of the skull behind the eye sockets. One of these windows is high on the roof of the skull, the other is down on the side of the cheek. These openings may be to make the skull lighter. They also provide areas for the jaw muscles to attach on to the skull, making it stronger and more powerful. In birds, the two openings have largely disappeared. Mammals have only one opening on each side, not two, while turtles have no openings at all.

red-tailed boa

▲ REPTILE PREDATOR

Snakes are also scaly, meat-eating reptiles, but they catch prey in very different ways from a crocodilian. They have delicate bodies and need to overpower prey quickly before it can inflict an injury. Some, such as this boa, squeeze their prey to death in their powerful coils. Others kill their prey with a poisonous bite.

Did you know? The sex of baby turtles, like crocodilians, depends on temperature.

▶ MONSTROUS LIZARD

The gila monster of North America is a lizard with small, bead-like scales. It is one of the world's two poisonous lizards, and its bright colors are a warning sign of its poisonous nature. The poison is produced in glands in the bottom jaw and chewed into both predators and prey. Crocodilians have much larger scales than lizards, and none are poisonous.

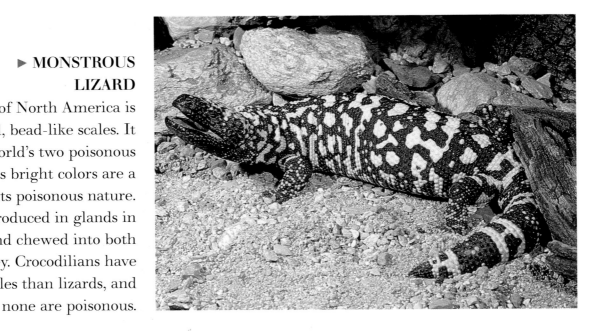

Living with People

Many people only ever see a crocodile or an alligator in a book or magazine, on television or at the cinema. These crocodilians are often huge, fierce monsters that attack and eat humans. Such images have given crocodilians a bad name. A few large crocodile types, such as the Nile and saltwater species, can be very dangerous, but most are timid creatures that are no threat to humans. Some people even keep baby crocodilians as pets. Humans are a much bigger threat to crocodilians than they are to us. People hunt them for their skins to make handbags, shoes and belts. Traditional Asian medicines are made from many of their body parts. Their bones are ground up to add to fertilizers and animal feed. Their meat and eggs are cooked and eaten, while perfume is made from their sex organs, musk and urine.

▲ ALLIGATOR DANGER
The barely visible head of an American alligator reinforces why swimming is not allowed. Alligators lurking under the water do occasionally attack people. This usually only happens when humans have invaded their habitat or disturbed nests or hatchlings.

► CROCODILE DUNDEE
One of the most dangerous and aggressive crocodilians is the saltwater crocodile, which appeared in the film *Crocodile Dundee.* In the film, Mick "Crocodile" Dundee saves an American journalist from a surprise attack by a saltie. An adult saltie can grow up to 23 ft long and is likely to view a human entering its territory as a possible meal.

58

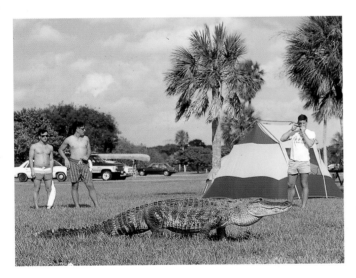

Krindlekrax

In Philip Ridley's 1991 story, Krindlekrax, a baby crocodile from a zoo escapes into a sewer and grows enormous on a diet of discarded toast. It becomes the mysterious monster Krindlekrax, which lurks beneath the pavements of Lizard Street. It is eventually tamed by the hero of the book, Ruskin Splinter, who wedges a medal down the crocodile's throat. He agrees to take the medal out if Krindlekrax will go back to the sewer and never come back to Lizard Street again.

▲ SKINS FOR SALE

These saltwater crocodile skins are being processed for tanning. Tanning converts the hard, horny, preserved skin into soft, flexible leather that can be made into bags, wallets, shoes and other goods. Some of the most valuable skins come from saltwater crocodiles, because they have small scales that have few bony plates inside.

▲ ALLIGATOR STROLL

An American alligator walks through a campsite, giving the campers a close-up view. Attacks on land are unlikely—the element of surprise is lost, and alligators cannot move fast out of the water. Meetings like this are harmless.

a false, glass eye has been inserted into the head

▶ TOURIST SOUVENIRS

A baby Siamese crocodile was killed so that its head could be made into a key ring as a tourist souvenir. Most tourists never manage to see a wild crocodilian, but if they buy souvenirs such as this, it means more animals will be killed for a cruel trade.

Rare Crocodilians

Almost half of all of crocodilian species are endangered, even though there is much less hunting today than in the past. Until the 1970s, five to ten million crocodilians were being killed each year—far too many for them to reproduce and build up their numbers again. Today, the loss of habitat is a greater threat than hunting for most crocodiles. Other problems include illegal hunting, trapping for food and medicine and the harvesting of crocodile eggs. Many species are not properly protected in national parks, and there are not enough crocodilians being reared on farms and ranches to make sure each species does not disappear forever. The four most endangered species are the Chinese alligator and the Philippine, Siamese and Orinoco crocodiles. Other species that only live in small populations are the Cuban crocodile, the black caiman and the gharial.

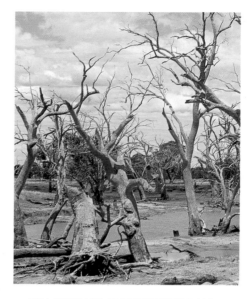

▲ **HABITAT DESTRUCTION**
The trees beside this billabong in Australia have died because there is too much salt in the water. Farmers removed many of the bush plants, which used to trap salt and stop it from sinking down into the ground. Now much of the land is ruined by high levels of salt, and it is difficult for crocodilians and other wildlife to live there.

▶ **FISHING COMPETITION**
People fishing for sport as well as for food create competition for crocodilians in some areas. They may also accidentally trap crocodilians underwater in their fishing nets causing them to drown. In waterways that are used for recreation, such as angling, bathing and boating, crocodilians may be accidentally killed by the blades of a motorboat's engine or intentionally killed because they may pose a threat to human life.

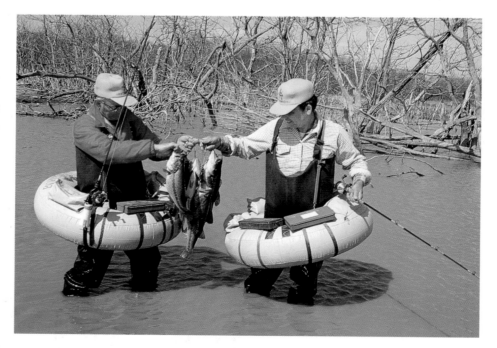

◄ CUBAN CROCODILE
This crocodile has the smallest range of any living crocodilian and is seriously endangered. It lives only on the island of Cuba and the nearby Isle of Pines. The growth of charcoal burning has drastically reduced the habitat of the Cuban crocodile. It has also moved into coastal areas and rivers, where it is more in danger from hunters.

Cuban crocodile
(*Crocodylus rhombifer*)

► SIAMESE CROCODILE
This endangered crocodile has almost died out in the wild. It was once found over large areas of Southeast Asia, but wild Siamese crocodiles now live only in Thailand. They have become so rare because of extensive hunting and habitat destruction. They now survive mainly on crocodile farms.

▲ ILLEGAL HUNTING
This poacher has speared a caiman in the Brazilian rainforest. Hunting crocodilians is banned in many countries, but people still hunt illegally in order to make money. Their hides are so valuable that, even though this caiman's skin contains many bony scutes, the soft parts will bring a good price.

▼ UNWANTED CROCODILE
A small saltwater crocodile that strayed into somebody's garden is captured so it can be returned to the wild. Its jaws are bound together with rope to stop it from biting the ranger. One of the biggest problems for crocodilians is the fact that more and more people want to live in the same places that they do.

Focus

WELL ADAPTED

Gharials have a light-colored, slender body with extensive webbing between the toes on the back feet. Their long back legs are relatively weak. Gharials are well adapted for life in the water but are not fast swimmers.

The gharial of northern India and the false gharial of Southeast Asia are both endangered species. Their numbers have fallen due to hunting for their skins, habitat loss and competition for their main food, fish. Many of the fast-flowing rivers in which they live have been dammed to provide water for crops and to generate electricity. Dams flood some areas and reduce the flow of water in others, as well as damaging the river banks where gharials nest. People collect their eggs for food and believe them to have medicinal properties. To save the gharial, young are reared in captivity and released into the wild. The false gharial, however, does not breed well in captivity.

CAPTIVE SURVIVAL

This gharial was bred in captivity and has been released into the wild. It has a radio tag on its tail so that scientists can follow its movements. In the 1970s, there were only about 300 wild gharials left. Captive breeding has increased the number to over 1,500.

MEAL TIME

A gharial lunges sideways to snap up a meal from a passing school of fish. Predatory catfish are a favorite meal. When gharial numbers went down, more catfish survived to eat the tilapia fish that local villagers caught for food.

on Gharials

FALSE IDENTITY

The false gharial looks like the true gharial and is probably related to it. It lives farther south than the true gharial, from southern Thailand to Borneo and Sumatra. In the wild, adults do not seem to help their young escape from the nest, and many die as they fend for themselves after hatching. Habitat loss and an increase in land used for rice farming have made false gharials rare. In Indonesia, over-collection of juveniles for rearing on farms may also have reduced numbers.

SAFE HOUSE

A scientist collects gharial eggs so that they can be protected in a sanctuary. There no predators will be able to get at them, and the temperature can be kept just right for development. In the wild, about 40 percent of eggs are destroyed by predators. Only about 1 percent of the young survive to adulthood.

WATER SPORT

In the dry, low-water months of winter, gharials spend a lot of time basking on sand banks. Even so, they are the most aquatic crocodilian. They move awkwardly when leaving the water and do not seem able to do the high walk like other crocodilians. Female gharials do not carry their young to the water. This is probably because their snouts are too slender and delicate and their teeth too sharp.

Conservation

Although people are frightened of crocodilians, they are a vital part of the web of life in tropical lands. They dig water holes that help other animals survive in dry seasons and clean up the environment by eating dead animals. Scientists find them interesting because they are good at fighting disease and rarely develop cancers. They are also fascinating to everyone as survivors from a prehistoric lost world. We need to find out more about their lives in the wild so we can help them to survive in the future. Some species, such as the American alligator, the saltwater crocodile and Johnston's crocodile of Australia and the gharial, have already been helped by conservation measures. Much more work needs to be done, however, such as preserving their habitats, stopping illegal poaching and smuggling, breeding rare species in captivity and releasing them into the wild.

▲ CROCODILE FARMS
Tourists watch a wrestler show off his skill at a crocodile farm. The farm breeds crocodiles for their skins, attracting tourists as extra income. Farms help stop crocodiles from being taken from the wild. The Samutprakan Crocodile Farm in Thailand has helped to save the rare Siamese crocodile from dying out by breeding them in captivity.

► RESEARCH REFUGE
Research at the Rockefeller Wildlife Refuge in Louisiana helped determine the best way of rearing American alligators in captivity. They are brought up in special hothouses where temperature, humidity, diet, space and disease can be controlled. They have piped music so they will be less disturbed by outside noises. In these conditions, the alligators grow more than 3 ft a year—much faster than in the wild.

► CAIMAN CONSERVATION

The tag on the foot of a black caiman helps identify it once it has been released into the wild. If the animal is caught again, it can be measured and weighed and the figures compared with previous records. This shows how well the animal is surviving in the wild.

▲ INTO THE FUTURE

This boy from Guyana is holding a baby dwarf caiman. Small numbers of caimans are sold as exotic pets. If people are paid more money for a living specimen than a dead one, they are less likely to kill crocodiles for skins. Educating people about why crocodilians are important is an important way of ensuring their future.

► RANCHING AND FARMING

A Nile crocodile is fed at a breeding station in South Africa. Crocodilians grow well on ranches or farms where they are fed properly. These places also provide information about the biology, health and feeding patterns of the reptiles.

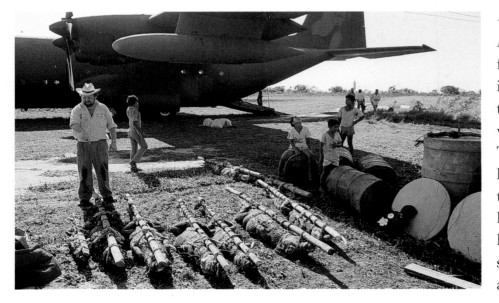

◄ A NEW HOME

A row of black caimans, saved from a ranching development in Bolivia, wait to be flown to the Beni Biosphere Reserve, where they will be protected. The number of black caimans has dropped dramatically, and the animals they used to eat have thrived as a result. This has caused problems for people, such as capybaras eating crops and piranhas attacking cattle.

LIZARDS

Lizards are a very diverse group of reptiles, but most are small, agile insect-eaters with good eyesight, four legs and a long tail. The smallest lizard is just ⅝in long. Some burrowing lizards have lost their legs and look more like snakes than lizards. The bodies of many lizards are decorated with spines, horns, frills or other structures, which they use for defense or attracting a mate. Lizards live all over the world, and house geckos have even moved into our homes.

Top Reptiles

Lizards form the largest group of reptiles—there are nearly 4,000 different species known. They are found in more places than any other type of reptile, and live everywhere, from deserts to the Arctic tundra, and exposed mountain slopes to isolated islands. A lizard's habitat can be anything from the highest branches in a forest's trees to the soil underneath its leaf litter. Like all living reptiles, lizards are cold-blooded, which means that their body temperature varies with that of their surroundings. Most are small and feed on insects, but some have become large, dangerous carnivores. A few eat only plants. Lizards are very varied in shape and color. Most have four legs, but some have lost their legs and look like snakes.

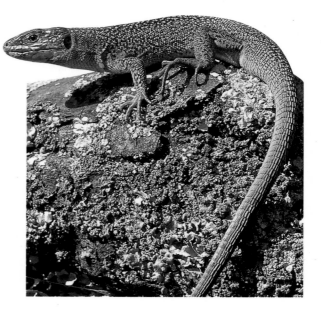

▲ **FIVE TOES, FOUR LEGS**
This green lizard is a typical lizard. It is active by day and has four legs, each with five toes. Most lizards are fairly small; in the food chain, they sit between insects and the predatory birds, mammals, and snakes.

▼ **LIZARD EGGS**
Reptiles lay their eggs on land. Their eggs are cleidoic, which means "closed-box"—the baby develops inside the egg, isolated from the outside world and often protected by a tough, leathery shell. Nutrition is supplied by the yolk sac, and waste products are stored in a membrane called the allantois. The amnion, a protective, fluid-filled membrane, surrounds the growing baby lizard and the yolk sac.

▲ **SCALY SKIN**
Lizards are covered in scales made of a substance called keratin, which is also the basis of human hair. Lizard scales vary in size, from the tiny grainlike scales on geckos to the large, fingernail-like scales, or scutes, of plated lizards. Scales offer protection from injury and against drying out.

MEGA MONITORS ▶

Lizards first appeared 100–150 million years ago. *Megalania priscus* was a giant Australian monitor lizard that would have made a Komodo dragon, the world's largest living lizard, look very puny. Adults reached 23 ft and may have weighed more than half a ton. They probably ate prehistoric kangaroos and giant wombats. *Megalania* lived until 25,000 years ago, and they may have met Australia's first humans.

23 ft

6 ft

Megalania priscus

10 ft

man

Komodo dragon

◀ GIANT DRAGONS

The heaviest lizard in the world is the Komodo dragon from the group of islands of the same name in Indonesia. Although there are stories of 16½-ft-long Komodo dragons, the longest specimen ever accurately measured was 10 ft. It can weigh up to 155 lbs. The Salvador's monitor lizard from New Guinea, a more slimline and lighter relative, may grow longer, to over 13 ft.

MINI MARVELS ▶

The Nosy Be pigmy chameleon from Northern Madagascar grows to no more than 1⅜ in long, but it is not the smallest living lizard. Even smaller is the Jaragua gecko from the Dominican Republic in the Caribbean. It grows to a maximum length of just ⅝ in and was discovered in 2001. It is the world's smallest lizard and the smallest land-living vertebrate (animal with a backbone) known to science.

Lizard Relatives

The first reptiles appeared on Earth over 260 million years ago. Most types that lived in the distant past, such as dinosaurs and flying pterodactyls, are extinct today. Even so the Class Reptilia currently contains over 7,000 living species, ranging from turtles to crocodiles and geckos to snakes. All reptiles have scaly or leathery protective skin, which allows them to survive in salty, hot or dry conditions that would kill many other animals. Most lay leathery-shelled eggs, but a few lizards and snakes bear live young —an adaptation to living in colder climates where eggs would die. This versatility makes reptiles excellent survivors. Even though we now live in the Age of Mammals, reptiles are still a very successful group.

▲ RELATION WITH A SHELL
Turtles and tortoises belong to an ancient order of reptiles that split from the main reptile line shortly after the ancestors of mammals did. They are distantly related to other modern reptiles—in fact, lizards are related less to turtles and tortoises than they are to dinosaurs or birds. Turtles live in the sea and fresh water, while tortoises live on land.

▲ DINOSAUR DINNER
In this reconstruction, a plant-eating *Iguanodon* is being stalked by two meat-eating *Deinonychus*. Although dinosaurs might look like giant lizards they were more closely related to crocodiles and birds. Unlike modern reptiles, many dinosaurs walked on two legs. Most of these ancient reptiles were plant-eaters but some ate meat.

▲ FIERCE HUNTER
Crocodiles and alligators include the largest reptiles alive today. Nile crocodiles such as this can grow to 20 ft long and weigh almost a ton, and the Indo-Pacific crocodile is even larger. Crocodilians eat meat and spend most of their time in water. They are distantly related to lizards and, like all egg-laying reptiles, they lay eggs on land.

Congo Monster

People living in the Congo rainforest claim it is inhabited by a giant Diplodocus-*like creature that they call Mokele-mbembe. Do dinosaurs still walk the Earth or could the monster be a large monitor lizard standing on its hind feet and stretching out its long neck? Several expeditions have set out in search of Mokele-mbembe but the mystery remains unsolved.*

THE FAMILY TREE ▼

As this tree shows, reptiles are a very diverse group. Turtles split away from the main reptilian line millions of years ago. Reptiles then divided into two main groups. The Archosauria (ancient reptiles) became dinosaurs, crocodilians, and birds. The Lepidosauria (scaled reptiles) includes tuataras, and modern lizards, snakes, and amphisbaenians (worm-lizards).

▲ TWO TUATARAS

These reptiles live on islands off the coast of New Zealand. Although they look like lizards, they have their own reptile group. They have hardly changed their appearance and behavior since dinosaurs walked the Earth. Only two species of tuatara are alive in the world today.

▼ LEGLESS LIZARDS

Amphisbaenians, or worm-lizards, are legless reptiles that evolved from lizards. There are around 130 species, living in Florida, northwestern Mexico, the West Indies, South America, Africa, and Mediterranean Europe. Burrowers in soil and sand, amphisbaenians feed on earthworms and other invertebrates.

tetrapods

amphibians

turtles and tortoises

mammal-like reptiles

mammals

Archosauria (thecodonts)

birds

crocodilians

dinosaurs

Lepidosauria

Squamata

tuataras

hard-tongued lizards

all other lizards

Iguania

amphisbaenians

snakes

The Iguania

Lizards are split into two main groups. The first of these is known to scientists as the Iguania, and contains over 1,300 species, including iguanas, agamas, chameleons, anoles, swift lizards, lava lizards, basilisks, and spiny lizards. The Iguania is an ancient group of reptiles that dates back almost 100 million years. It is split into two smaller groups, because agamas and chameleons have different teeth and live on different continents to iguanas and most of their relatives. Although some agamas look like iguanas, this is because they have become alike as a result of having similar lifestyles, and not because they are closely related.

▲ AMAZING AGAMAS

There are 300 species of agama, living in southeastern Europe, Asia, Africa, and Australia. Many agamas are sun lovers, and include desert-dwellers such as the frilled lizards and this eastern bearded dragon. This family also contains the tiny flying lizards of Southeast Asia and the secretive rain forest dragons of New Guinea and Queensland in Australia.

COLOR-CHANGING CHAMELEONS ▶
This veiled chameleon comes from the Yemen, on the Arabian Peninsula. With their "turret-eyes," curly prehensile tails, famous color-changing capabilities, and long, sticky tongues, the chameleons must be the strangest family of lizards in the world. Although most of the 160 species live in Africa and Madagascar, the Indian chameleon comes from southern Asia, and the European chameleon is found in southern Spain and Crete.

Did you know? Chameleons can change the color of their skin to match their surroundings.

IGUANAS AND CHUCKWALLAS ▶

Most iguanas, and their close relatives, the chuckwallas, live in the Americas. Many are found in the West Indies, including the powerful rhinoceros iguanas. The Central and South American green iguana is perhaps the most familiar lizard in the world, but not all iguanas are American. The iguana on the right is from Fiji, in the Pacific Ocean.

▲ NATIVE KNIGHTS

The knight anole is a native of Cuba, but it was introduced to southern Florida in 1952. There it hunts down the smaller green anole, which has become an endangered species in Florida, although it lives in many other parts of the world, including Hawaii. There are about 400 species of anoles in South America and the West Indies.

SWIFT SPECIES ▶

This Cuvier's Malagasy swift lives in the dry scrub and rocky outcrops of Madagascar, a large island off the eastern coast of Africa. In all, seven insect-eating species of small, tree- and rock-dwelling swifts live there. They lay four to six eggs. Another family of small fast-moving lizards known as swifts come from the Americas, from the U.S.A. down to Argentina.

DASHING BASILISKS ▶

The plumed basilisk is the largest species of basilisk. The four species, together with the helmeted and cone-headed lizards, make up a small, rain forest-dwelling family that comes from Central America and northern South America. They are sometimes called "Jesus lizards", because they can dash across water for some distance before breaking the surface.

OUT OF AFRICA

Jackson's three-horned chameleon inhabits woodland on the slopes of Africa's Mount Kenya, but can also be found in the suburbs of Kenya's capital city, Nairobi. Males have longer horns than females. Small populations have become established on the Hawaiian Islands after pet Jackson's chameleons were released.

GIANT OF THE FORESTS

Parson's chameleon can reach 27 in long. This giant from Madagascar is the second-largest chameleon, after Oustalet's chameleon, which also comes from Madagascar. Parson's chameleon is an inhabitant of the island's wet eastern forest, and it rarely changes color.

Focus on

When most people think of a chameleon, they imagine a big, color-changing lizard with horns. This "typical chameleon" image does not do justice to this diverse family of lizards. Most of the 160 or so species are split fifty-fifty between Africa and Madagascar, but there is also a species in southern Europe, one on the Arabian Peninsula and another in India. Not all chameleons live in rain forests—many inhabit dry woodland and some are found in deserts. The idea of chameleons being green lizards that can change color is also a generalization—some of the smaller species are brown and they cannot change their color at all.

EASTERN COLOR

The Southeast Asian chameleon, or Indian chameleon, is found from Pakistan and India to northern parts of Sri Lanka. The only truly Asian chameleon, it lives in dry forests and woodland. It lays up to 30 eggs in early winter. Although winter might seem a strange time to lay eggs, this is actually the dry season where this chameleon lives.

Chameleons

FIT TO DROP

Its short tail, brown pigmentation and dark lines make the West African leaf chameleon look like a dead leaf hanging from a twig. It does not change color. If it is disturbed, it just falls to the ground and lies still, blending in with the dead brown leaves on the forest floor. This small lizard reaches maturity in three months, and it feeds on termites, which it finds on the short, rain forest shrubs where it lives.

DESERT DWELLER

Chameleons are usually associated with rain forest and woodland, but some species live in the desert. The Namaqua chameleon is found in the arid regions of Namibia and western South Africa. It spends most of its time on the ground, but will climb up on rocks and into bushes to keep cool. The Namaqua chameleon has a large mouth and eats all kinds of animals, from insects to small lizards and snakes.

FAST DEVELOPERS

Natal dwarf chameleons live in dry thickets and gardens in South Africa. Males vary in color and may be bright blue or red. Females and juveniles are gray, brown, or green. The Natal chameleon gives birth to between eight and twenty live babies. These youngsters grow fast and can have babies of their own by the time they are nine months old. Such rapid development is a characteristic of many chameleons.

Hard Tongues

All lizards not contained in the Iguania belong to a group known as the Scleroglossa, or hard-tongued lizards. Their tongues are tough and flat. There are more than 2,700 species of hard-tongued lizard, ranging in size from the tiny insectivorous Caribbean least geckos to large carnivorous monitor lizards. Many of the 17 families have become burrowers and have lost their legs, after millions of years of them getting smaller and smaller to make burrowing easier. Hard-tongued lizards are the ancestors of amphisbaenians and snakes. They include a huge variety of species, among them geckos, lacertid lizards, zonures, skinks, anguid lizards, and monitor lizards.

▲ STICKY FINGERS

Most geckos are nocturnal and hunt insects. The larger species, such as this tokay gecko, include other lizards in their diet. Geckos are well known for their ability to walk up walls and tree trunks, and across ceilings. They do this with the help of flattened toes that have special plates called scansors underneath. Not all geckos can climb like this, however.

SUN LOVERS ▶

Europe's eyed lizard preys on many smaller lizards, insects, and spiders. Like most of the lizards that are commonly seen in Europe, it belongs to the lacertid family. Indeed the green lizards, wall lizards, and ruin lizards often seen basking in the sun are all lacertids. The most widespread European species is the viviparous lizard. Other lacertids live in Africa and Asia. All lacertids are active and alert hunters of insects and spiders.

◄ **REAR GUARD**

The sungazer is the largest of the zonures, which are also called girdled lizards because their spiny scales are arranged in rings, or girdles, around the body. The sungazer has extremely spiny scales on its tail. The scales are used to defend the lizard when it dives headfirst down a hole or wedges itself into a rocky crevice.

SMOOTHLY DOES IT ►

Most skinks, including this Müller's skink, have smooth shiny scales. Skinks make up the largest lizard family. Most skinks are small, active by day, live on the ground, and eat insects. However, the Solomon's monkey-tail skink breaks all the rules by being a tree-living plant-eater that is active by night.

▲ **WORM, SNAKE, OR LIZARD?**

The European slowworm is a legless lizard that feeds on slugs and other soft-bodied creatures. It is the best-known anguid lizard, but not all anguids lack limbs—the American alligator lizards have short legs, but they still wriggle along. The longest anguid is the 3-ft European glass lizard. It looks like a snake, but it is a true lizard with eyelids and ear openings.

▲ **ALMOST INVISIBLE**

This Indo-Malay water monitor is almost invisible against the rock it is lying on. Like other monitor lizards, it is a good climber and swimmer. They are found in Africa and Asia, but most live in Australia, and range in size from the 10-in-long short-tailed monitor to the giant Komodo dragon. Most eat insects or vertebrates but Gray's monitor also eats fruit.

Amphisbaenians

The amphisbaenians, also known as worm lizards, are a group of reptiles that evolved from lizards. Worm lizards have tiny eyes that are covered by transparent scales, and rely mainly on taste, smell, and hearing to find their way around. They are found in Florida, the West Indies, Mexico, South America, southern Europe, the Middle East, and Africa. Although they are widely distributed, worm lizards are not very well understood because they are rarely seen. They are secretive burrowers and resemble earthworms. Most species can discard their tails in defense, but they cannot grow new ones, unlike many true lizards. Most worm lizards lay eggs, although a few bear live young. All feed on soft-bodied invertebrates, such as worms and insect larvae (young).

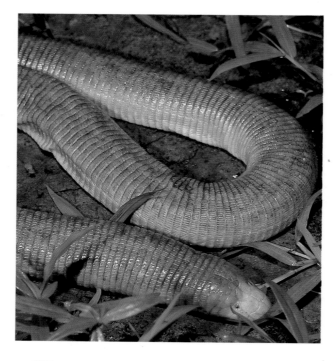

▲ **WHITE GIANT**

The largest amphisbaenian is the white worm lizard of South America. It can grow to at least 22 in long and has a pointed snout and a blunt, rounded tail. It hunts deep in the nests of leaf-cutting ants. The white worm lizard follows ant trails back to the nest and enters the refuse area deep below the ants' carefully cultured fungus gardens. Once it is there, it feeds on beetle larvae.

◄ **ANT EATER**

Black and white worm lizards live in South America in the Amazon rain forest. It is a large species—like the white worm lizard—and it can reach up to 12 in long. The black and white worm-lizard's striking pattern contrasts with its light pink head, which is usually marked with a single, central black spot. This species lives in ant nests, where it lays its eggs and feeds mainly on ant larvae and pupae. It is seen above ground only after heavy rain.

WEIRD AND WONDERFUL ▼

The ajolates, or mole worm lizards, are among the strangest of all reptiles. Like other worm lizards, they have elongated bodies covered with rings of small rectangular scales. The three known species of mole worm lizards also have a pair of front feet for digging. Mole worm lizards inhabit sandy, low-lying country in Mexico. Their bodies have a long fold running from one end to the other. This fold may allow the body to expand when they feed and breathe.

Did you know? In Greek myths the amphisbaenia was a monstrous snake with a head at each end.

◄ SOLE EUROPEAN

Europe's only amphisbaenian is the Iberian worm lizard, which lives in Spain and Portugal. It has close relatives in Morocco. Usually black, brown, or yellow, with a paler underside and sometimes speckled with pink, at first sight, this species looks like an earthworm. However, a closer examination will reveal a specialized, pointed head for burrowing, a mouth with a short tongue, and tiny, faint eyes. The body is ringed with rows of tiny, square scales. Rarely seen above ground, this species is found under flat stones and in leaf litter in sandy woodland, and it feeds on a wide variety of insects.

◄ TOP TUNNELER

The checkered worm lizard inhabits open rocky country and woodland in North Africa. It has a slightly pointed head and a stout body patterned with dark brown spots on a lighter background. When it is threatened, the checkered worm lizard may roll into a ball. This species belongs to the most advanced family of worm lizards, which have developed specialized techniques for tunnel excavation.

Where in the World

Lizards are the most numerous of all reptiles, and they are also among the most adaptable—they live in regions where even snakes are absent. Lizards have adapted to cope with cold on mountains and inside the Arctic Circle and can endure the heat of any desert. They are excellent colonizers—especially those species that give birth to live young—and can adapt in time to feed on anything that is available. In fact, almost everywhere you look on land, there is a good chance a lizard lives there. Unlike amphibians, which lived on Earth before reptiles, some lizards have learned to live in or near the sea, and have adapted to high levels of salt in their diets.

▲ DUSTY DESERT
Many lizards live in deserts but surviving there is hard. Desert lizards are often nocturnal to avoid the heat. They rarely drink, and many survive on the water they get from their food alone. Some desert lizards, such as this Namib gecko, have webbed feet or fringes on their toes to help them run over sand.

▲ ICY COLD
The Arctic is not an ideal place for reptiles, but a few lizards do live in this cold region and are active in the short summers. The viviparous lizard is common throughout Europe, but unlike other European lizards, it is also found well inside the Arctic Circle. Viviparous means live-bearing, and most reptiles that live in cold climates give birth to live young.

▲ SEASHORE SALT
The swollen-snouted, side-blotch lizard is one of the few lizards that live on the seashore. It lives on the tiny island of Isla Coloradito, off Mexico, where it eats shore-living crustaceans called slaters and the sea lice that infest the sea lion colony. The salt level in its diet is 20 times the lethal level of other lizards. Special glands in its nostrils help it get rid of some of the salt.

◄ WHERE DO LIZARDS LIVE?

Arctic Circle

EUROPE

NORTH AMERICA

ASIA
The Himalayas

Mexico

AFRICA

New Guinea

SOUTH AMERICA

Namibia

AUSTRALIA

lizards live on every continent except the Antarctic

Lizards inhabit every continent apart from Antarctica, and have colonized most island groups. Some species, such as house geckos, have even used human transportation to reach and colonize islands a long way from land. Lizards are not found in areas of very high altitude and latitude, because it is too cold for them. The five species shown on these two pages are from different continents and different habitats. The only thing these lizards have in common is that they all survive in difficult conditions.

MOUNTAIN HIGH ►

The mountains are tough places for reptiles, which rely on the sun to keep them warm and active. Few lizards can survive in these conditions, but one exception is the rock agama from the southern Himalayas. It is found as high as 7,500 ft, basking on rocks along the freezing rivers that pour from glaciers. The rock agama hibernates in winter to save energy and avoid the worst of the cold.

◄ STEAMY RAIN FOREST

Lizards are everywhere in rain forests: in the canopy, on the tall trunks, down on the ground and underneath the leaf litter. There is plenty of food in the forest, but there are also plenty of predators, so lizards have to be alert. New Guinea's twin-crested anglehead lizard lives in rain forests, but it is seldom seen because it is well camouflaged.

A Marine

The marine iguana of the Galapagos Islands off Ecuador is the only truly oceangoing lizard in the world. It lives its entire life along the coast, never venturing far inland, and it survives on a diet of seaweed and the droppings of seals and crabs, which provide bacteria to aid its digestion. This diet results in dangerously high levels of salt entering the lizard's body. To avoid being poisoned, marine iguanas get rid of the salt with loud snorts, spraying the white particles of salt on the rocks, themselves, and their neighbors. A typical day for a marine iguana is spent mostly basking in the sun and feeding.

SUNBATHERS

Basking is very important to marine iguanas, especially the males, which dive into the cold waters to feed. Without basking, they would be unable to warm up enough for their bodies to digest their food. Basking marine iguanas must be alert for predators. Snakes and birds of prey will kill small iguanas if they can catch them.

UNDERWATER BREAKFAST

Female and young marine iguanas forage for food on the exposed rocks at low tide, but the adult males are more adventurous. They dive into the water and swim down to the submerged seaweed beds to browse. Large males can dive as deep as 33 ft in search of a meal.

HEAD TO HEAD

Male marine iguanas do not fight over feeding grounds, but they do disagree over mating territories. A mating territory is an area where an adult male has a good chance of meeting and courting females. These small patches of rock are disputed with body postures, head bobs, gaping mouths, and head-butting, until one male gives in and leaves.

Iguana's Day

GROUP LIVING

Marine iguanas are unusual for large lizards—they gather together at night to sleep in groups, like sea lions. They even manage to sleep piled on top of each other. Marine iguanas are much less territorial than land iguanas, so fights do not break out over sleeping areas. By sleeping huddled together, they conserve energy and cool down more slowly than if they slept alone.

COURTSHIP FINERY

During the breeding season, the male marine iguana develops large patches of red, and sometimes green skin, which is in strong contrast to his usual black or dark-gray color. At this time, he is interested in mating with as many females as possible, and spends a lot of his time trying to fight off smaller males and compete with larger males for mating territories.

ALL AT SEA

To get from one rocky outcrop to another, or to reach the deeper, richer feeding grounds, the marine iguana must venture into the sea. These lizards are extremely strong swimmers, powered by muscular tails, and this is essential because currents around the Galapagos are very strong.

Bone and Cartilage

The scaffolding that supports a lizard's body is called bone. This is a living tissue that develops as a lizard matures from juvenile to adult. In hatchlings, the body is supported by flexible cartilage. As a lizard ages, calcium is deposited in the cartilage and it hardens, thickens, and becomes bone. Lizards obtain calcium from their food. Different lizards have different skeletons, and scientists have divided lizards into families based mostly on skeletal features and the way bones develop.

backbone

rib cage

skull

▲ LIZARD SKELETON

Most lizards have four legs, each ending in five toes. As with all reptiles, the body is supported by the backbone, which stretches from the neck to the tail. The backbone is actually not one bone but many small bones, or vertebrae. Important organs, such as the heart and lungs, are protected by the rib cage. The skull forms a tough case around the brain.

▼ FASCINATING HORNS

Many lizards have extra structures that stick out from their body. Johnston's chameleon has three large horns on the front of its head. The horns are made of soft tissue, and they grow from raised structures on the skull. All Johnston's chameleons have these horns, but they are larger on males than females. Males use their horns to intimidate rivals, and they may also be helpful in attracting a female mate.

▲ LOST LIMBS

Some lizards have less than five toes; others have lost all their limbs. Scaly-feet lizards have completely lost their front legs, and all that remains of their hind limbs is a small scaly flap. Despite the small size of the scaly flaps, they are used for gripping and moving across rock.

monitor lizard skull

monkeytail skink skull
(*not to scale*)

acrodont teeth

pleurodont teeth

▲ SKULL AND TEETH

Monitor lizards, chameleons, iguanas, and agamas have their teeth on top of the jawbone, which is known as acrodont. Other lizards, such as the monkeytail skink, have pleurodont teeth, positioned on the side of the jawbone. The lower jawbones are linked to the back of the skull by a ball and socket joint.

Did you know? Many lizards are classified by the structure of the bones in their skull.

◄ DEFENSIVE UMBRELLA

When the Australian frilled lizard feels threatened, it opens its mouth. This action causes a wide frill of skin around its neck to open like an umbrella. The frill is supported by special bones but is poorly developed in juveniles. It is intended to frighten an enemy and give the lizard time to turn and run away. At rest, or when the lizard is running or climbing, the frill is folded along the body.

SPECIAL SAILS ►

Some lizards have a sail-like fin on their back. Supported by cartilage or bony extensions from the backbone, these fins may serve more than one purpose. In chameleons, they may aid balance or help with camouflage by making the lizard look more like a leaf. They also increase a lizard's body surface area to make it easier to warm up quickly in the sun.

Internal Anatomy

Although on the outside, lizards look much like other living creatures, under the skin all kinds of peculiar anatomical adaptations help make them successful. Lizards have special breath-holding abilities, extra sensory organs and telescopic (extendable) tongues. A few species even have green blood to protect them from parasites. Internal anatomy covers everything beneath the skin, from the skeleton and muscles to the organs and blood. It includes not only the bones, but also the muscles, tendons, and ligaments that let the skeleton move, and soft-tissue organs such as the brain, thoracic, and abdominal organs.

▲ DIVING HOUDINIS

When a green iguana that is basking over a river feels threatened, it may leap into the water, around 30 ft below, swim to the bottom, and stay there for up to 30 minutes. Iguanas can hold their breath and survive underwater like this by changing the flow of blood through the heart. Instead of sending blood from the body to the lungs, they pump it back through the body and use every bit of oxygen that is in it before they need to breathe again.

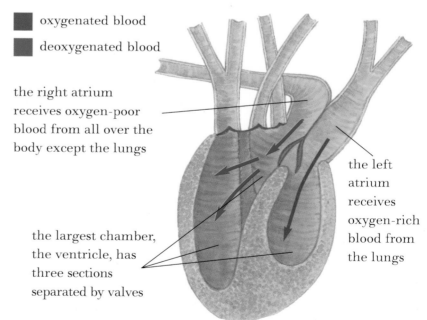

■ oxygenated blood

■ deoxygenated blood

the right atrium receives oxygen-poor blood from all over the body except the lungs

the left atrium receives oxygen-rich blood from the lungs

the largest chamber, the ventricle, has three sections separated by valves

▲ THREE-CHAMBERED HEART

A lizard's heart has three chambers, unlike ours, which has four. Two chambers, called the atria, receive blood from the body. Oxygen-rich blood from the left atrium is kept separate from oxygen-poor blood from the right.

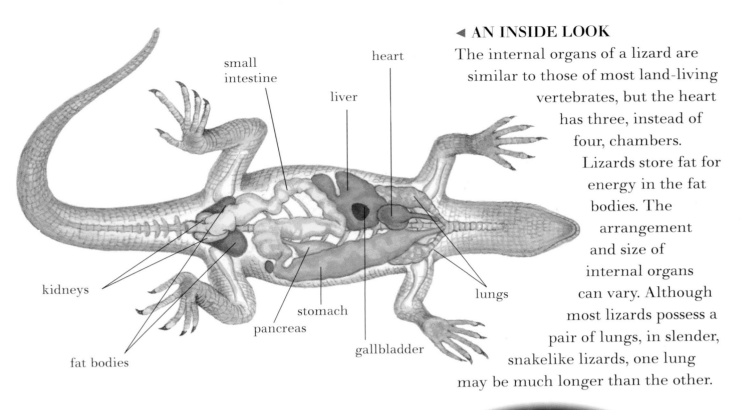

small intestine

heart

liver

kidneys

stomach

pancreas

fat bodies

gallbladder

lungs

◄ AN INSIDE LOOK

The internal organs of a lizard are similar to those of most land-living vertebrates, but the heart has three, instead of four, chambers. Lizards store fat for energy in the fat bodies. The arrangement and size of internal organs can vary. Although most lizards possess a pair of lungs, in slender, snakelike lizards, one lung may be much longer than the other.

TONGUE AND GROOVES ►

Lizards' tongues begin at the front of their mouths, as you can see in this photograph of a fat-tailed gecko's mouth. Mammals' tongues begin at the back of the throat. The open airway or glottis can be seen in the gecko's mouth. Forked-tongued lizards, such as monitors, have an extra organ, known as Jacobson's organ, which they use to analyze scent particles. The lizard places the tips of its tongue in two grooves in the roof of the mouth, which lead to the organ above.

◄ PROTECTIVE PIGMENT

Most lizards have red blood but one unusual group has blood that is green. Green-blooded skinks have a green pigment in their blood that would be poisonous to most animals. In the past it was thought that the skinks had this so that they would be unpleasant to eat. It is now believed the green pigment protects the skinks from blood parasites, such as the ones that cause malaria.

Skin and Scales

All reptiles have tough and almost completely waterproof skin. Lizard skin is made of three layers. The outer layer, or epidermis, is usually transparent and is shed regularly as the lizard grows. Under the epidermis is a layer called the stratum intermediate, which contains the pigments that give the lizard color. Beneath that is the inner layer, or dermis. In many hard-tongued lizards, this layer contains rigid plates called osteoderms ("bone skin"), which add strength to the skin. Scales vary in shape and texture from the smooth, rounded scales of skinks to the sharp, keeled (ridged) scales of zonures. Lizards don't have sweat glands as mammals do, but they have special glands between the scales.

▲ ARMOR PLATES

Plated lizards, such as this southern African, rough-scaled, plated lizard, have rectangular platelike scales arranged in regular overlapping rows around the body. These scales are strengthened by the presence of protective osteoderms (bony plates). Along each of the lizard's flanks is a long fold of skin containing small granular scales. This allows the lizard to expand its body when it breathes, in what would otherwise be a very constricting suit of armor.

SMOOTH AND SHINY ▶

This slowworm and many ground-dwelling skinks have bodies covered in small, rounded, smooth scales that give little resistance when the reptile is burrowing and moving underneath debris. The slowworm is legless so when it sheds its epidermis, the entire layer often comes off in one piece, not in several pieces like other lizards. The skin of the slowworm contains protective osteoderms.

▲ TINY BEADS

The Salvador's monitor lizard, which is a large, tree-climbing lizard from New Guinea, has numerous tiny scales. The smaller and more regular a lizard's scales are, the more flexible its body is. The Gila monster and beaded lizard have scales that look even more like beads.

▲ MOBILE FOLDS

The small scales of South America's northern tegu are arranged in a series of overlapping triangular folds. The northern tegu is a speedy hunter, and this arrangement of scale groups, which move over each other as the lizard runs, gives the tegu both protection and agility.

▲ SHARP RIDGES

The back of the Bosc monitor lizard from the African savannas has numerous interlocking but nonoverlapping, keeled scales. Those on the lizard's underside are smaller and not keeled. Keeled scales may help dew condense on the lizard's back at night, giving it water to drink in an otherwise arid environment.

▲ SCATTERED SCALES

Geckos have granular, velvety, or papery skin. The tokay gecko has scattered conical scales surrounded by smaller, granular scales. The skin of smaller geckos is usually much more fragile. One species from Madagascar sheds all three layers of its skin if it is grasped.

OFF WITH THE OLD ▶

Lizards must shed the outer layer of their skins in order to grow. Unlike snakes, they tend to shed their skin in pieces. This wonder gecko has begun to shed its old skin. Since the cells that produce pattern and color are in the second layer, the old skin looks colorless. The original colors are visible in the newly emerged gecko.

How Lizards

BROKEN GLASS

Many lizards can lose their tails for protection. This Australian scaly-foot has a long tail that can be quickly discarded if it is grasped. The European slowworm got its scientific name, *Anguis fragilis,* from the fact that it is "broken" easily. The scheltopusik got its other name, glass snake, because it is legless and has the habit of breaking its extremely long tail.

Small lizards often show their tails when they are threatened. Some species have bright-colored tails that, when combined with a tail-waving motion, attract a predator's attention and draw its attack away from the lizard's head and body. As a predator pounces on the lizard's tail, powerful muscular contractions in the tail make it snap off. The discarded tail thrashes around, so that the predator's attention is further distracted and the lizard can escape. The muscles at the severance point collapse and seal the tail's end to prevent blood loss. Soon the wound heals and the lizard grows a new tail.

broken tail

new tail

TAIL INTACT

The common house gecko has many enemies that would like to make a meal of it. This gecko has been lucky—it still has its original tail, but would be ready to sacrifice it in a minute if it was threatened by a predator. The original tail has a pattern like that on the body and has different scales on the top from those underneath.

THE ESCAPE MECHANISM

Lizards that can lose their tails have special breaking points built into them. When the tail is grasped, powerful muscular contractions will cause a fracture right through the tail, severing it at that point. The muscles then close the wound preventing further loss of blood.

Grow New Tails

A LOST TAIL

A lizard may try to escape being captured by losing its tail. At first, this house gecko's tail thrashes around vigorously, but it is now still and lying upside down. Since the muscle bundles in the injured base of the tail have collapsed to seal the wound, there has been little blood loss. Although the gecko may look strange without its tail, at least it is still alive and can escape from its enemy. It has survived its ordeal and can continue living. A new tail will grow to replace the one it has lost.

NEARLY AS GOOD AS NEW

This house gecko lost its tail some time ago and has now grown a new one. The new tail is supported not by bone, but by a rod of cartilage—the same material you have in the bridge of your nose. The new tail does not look as good as the old one, it looks like a cheap, extra part, but it does the job almost as well as the original.

A LIZARD WITH TWO TAILS

When a lizard loses only part of its tail, it can grow what is called a bifurcated tail. This house gecko escaped, with the original tail loosely attached to the body. Since the blood vessels survived, the original tail recovered. But another tail grew out from the open wound, resulting in a curious fork-tailed gecko.

Getting Around

The typical lizard has four well-developed legs, each with five clawed toes. The legs stick out from the side of the body. This means that the body is thrown into S-shaped curves when the lizard walks and runs. Lizard backbones are flexible to let the lizard move easily as its stride lengthens. Some lizards run very fast on all fours. Others run even faster using just their hind legs with the front of the body raised and the tail for balance. In tree-dwelling species, the feet and tail may be adapted for climbing.

▲ A FIFTH LIMB

Some tree-living lizards have prehensile tails, which they can use when climbing. The monkey-tail skink is a large lizard from the Solomon Islands that uses its powerful tail when clambering in the forest canopy.

▲ SPIDER MEN

Geckos are famous for their ability to run up walls and glass, but not all geckos can do this. Only the geckos with expanded digits, such as house geckos and tokay geckos, can climb sheer surfaces. Under their toes are a series of flattened plates called "scansors," which mean they can stick on to almost any flat surface.

▼ WALKING ON WATER

Basilisks escape predators by running very fast on their long-toed hind-limbs. They can sprint across water for quite awhile before they break the surface of the water and fall in. This unusual ability to run on water has earned them the nickname of "Jesus lizard." Some other long-legged lizards can also run on water.

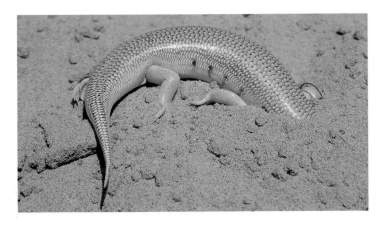

▲ LIFE UNDERGROUND

Many desert lizards spend part of their lives underground, escaping there from enemies and the heat of the sun. Africa's sand fish disappears into loose sand extremely rapidly, digging with its legs and flattened snout. Other lizards have developed an elongated body and lost their limbs, so that they can swim through the sand like eels in water.

▲ LEAP FOR FREEDOM

Flying lizards and flying geckos do not actually fly but glide down from trees to avoid predators. The flying gecko has webs of skin between its toes and also along the side of its body to slow its descent, but this flying lizard is more elaborate. It has a pair of "wings" spread out by false ribs to produce the lizard equivalent of a parachute.

Night Fighters

"Gecko" is an onomatopoeic word—a word that sounds like what it describes. This comes from the Malay word "gekok," which is derived from the noise that some geckos make when they call. The tokay gecko has another call that sounds like "tow-kay." Geckos are active after dark, and this led the Japanese to give the name "Gekkoh" to their night-fighter aircraft in World War II.

HOLDING ON ▶

Chameleons' toes are fused together. Each foot has three toes opposing two toes. The toes grip in the same way as a human's opposing thumb and other four fingers. This makes the chameleon such an expert climber that it can walk along slender twigs.

Sensing the Surroundings

Lizards have a variety of finely tuned sense organs to allow them to move around, locate and capture prey, avoid predators, and find a mate. Eyesight is an important sense for most lizards, but the structure of the retina (the back of the inside of the eye) varies a lot. The retinas of day-living lizards are dominated by cells called cones, giving them detailed vision, and those of nocturnal species have far more light-sensing rod cells, which increases their ability to see by moonlight. Lizards that are active at dusk and dawn have vertical pupils that close down to protect the sensitive retina from bright daylight. Day-living lizards may also possess color vision.

▲ EAGLE EYES

Lizards that are active by day, such as the green iguana, have excellent vision. Focusing for studying close detail is accomplished by changing the shape of the soft, deformable lens of the eye. Many lizards need to be able to focus rapidly, because they move around quickly and with agility, so that they can catch fast-moving insects. Vision is also important for basking lizards, since they must be able to locate approaching predators.

◄ LOOKING TWO WAYS AT ONCE

Chameleons are the only land vertebrates with eyes that move independently. This Parson's chameleon can use its turret-eyes to look in two directions at the same time. When an insect is located, both eyes converge on the prey and, working like a telephoto lens, they focus quickly and precisely to enlarge the image. The turret-eyes and the long sticky tongue evolved to work together, making chameleons expert shots when they shoot out their tongues to capture insects.

94

▼ A THIRD EYE

Green iguanas and many other lizards have a small circular object in the middle of their heads. This is the pineal eye, a third eye with a lens, retina, and a nerve feeding back into the brain, but it has no muscles, making it unable to focus. The pineal eye may help basking lizards to monitor how much sunlight they are receiving, but the way in which it works is not yet fully understood.

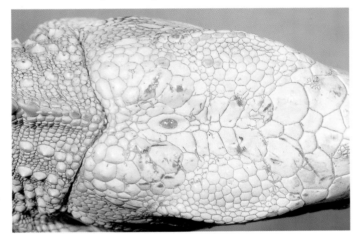

SEEK WITH FORKED TONGUE ▶

Some hard-tongued lizards have a Jacobson's organ that allows them to "taste" the air and track prey from a long way away. The forked tongue of this water monitor lizard is picking up odor particles and delivering them to the Jacobson's organ to be analyzed. The forks of the tongue help it tell direction—if more interesting particles are on the right fork, the lizard turns right.

▲ LISTENING LIZARDS

Lizard ears are made up of three parts: the outer, middle, and inner ear. The eardrum of this bearded dragon is visible on the side of its head, because the outer ear is absent. In other species, the eardrum is hidden by a deep, outer ear opening. Most lizards have external ears, but some have scales over them and others have no eardrum at all.

◀ PECULIAR TASTES

The herbivorous monkey-tail skink has a bulbous tongue with a slightly bi-lobed tip that contains many taste buds. This skink does not eat insects or meat so it does not have to track down any prey, but probably uses its sensitive tongue to discriminate between suitable and unsuitable leaves. Monkey-tail skinks are social lizards, and tongue-licking may also be a way of recognizing other members of the colony.

The Carnivores

Although the majority of lizards are either partly or totally carnivorous (meat-eating), even plant-eating lizards occasionally eat insects. Many lizards are active predators, hunting down their prey and capturing it with a lightning dash. Some meat-eating lizards take advantage of wounded, sick, dying, and dead animals for an easy meal. Animals that feed like this are called scavengers. Many lizards have a strong sense of smell and are able to locate prey that is hidden or buried. Komodo dragons are said to be able to smell prey from up to 2½ miles away. Other monitor lizards, and tegus, are experts at finding turtle and crocodile eggs, as well as the eggs of other lizards.

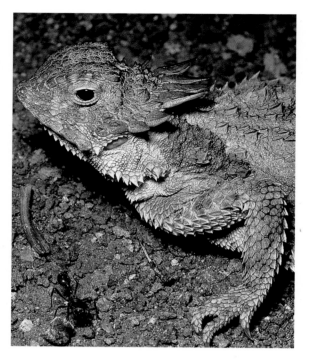

▲ MANY MINI MEALS

Ants are very small prey, but some lizards specialize in eating them. The horned lizards of North America's deserts are squat, spiny lizards that feed entirely on ants. Because ants are small, hundreds must be eaten at each meal. Fortunately for horned lizards, ants occur in large numbers and swarm together when their colony is attacked.

▲ PINPOINT ACCURACY

A chameleon, such as this panther chameleon, approaches its insect prey with stealth, focusing both eyes on the insect to judge how far away it is and extending its head forward as it gauges the moment to strike. Once the lizard is in position, it shoots out its long tongue rapidly and then pulls it back into its mouth with the insect stuck on the tip. Chameleons have prehensile tails, adapted for grasping, which help them grip twigs and branches when they are hunting.

Did you know? The chameleon's tongue is so long that it may be twice the length of its entire body.

▼ CRUSHING BITE

The swamp-dwelling caiman lizard from the Amazon rain forest looks a little like a crocodile. This excellent swimmer hunts aquatic snails underwater, which are crushed by flat teeth in the lizard's powerful jaws.

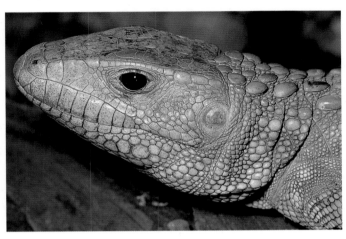

▲ DOWN IN ONE

Most legless lizards have tiny mouths and can only eat small prey. But Burton's snake lizard, a relative of Australia's geckos, specializes in eating skinks. Its jaws are much more flexible than those of other lizards, and its teeth curve backward, allowing it to swallow prey whole and head first in the same way a snake does.

◄ FEARLESS KILLER

Most monitor lizards are true all-around carnivores—they feed on small mammals, scavenge the carcasses of lion kills, and steal eggs from crocodile nests. Unlike most other animals, large monitors are not even afraid of snakes, and often feed on them. This Nile monitor is killing a sand snake, which is helpless against the monitor lizard's crushing jaws.

DANGEROUS PREY ►

Some lizards feed on very dangerous prey. North African desert agamas usually eat harmless insects, but sometimes they make a meal of a scorpion. To do this it must act quickly, and crush the scorpion in its powerful jaws before its tail can deliver its deadly sting.

Vegetarian Lizards

Plant-eating reptiles are rare, and only tortoises, and a few turtles and lizards, have a truly vegetarian diet. Many lizards that eat vegetation also eat insects and so are really omnivores (animals that eat plants and meat). Some lizards start life eating insects and only turn vegetarian when they become adults. Most plant-eating lizards feed on leaves, which are easy to find but hard to digest. Many leaf-eating lizards select only fresh, new shoots, which are easier to digest. Eating fruit is easier but less common in lizards, and a few species feed on seeds, flower heads, or nectar. Marine iguanas eat seaweed.

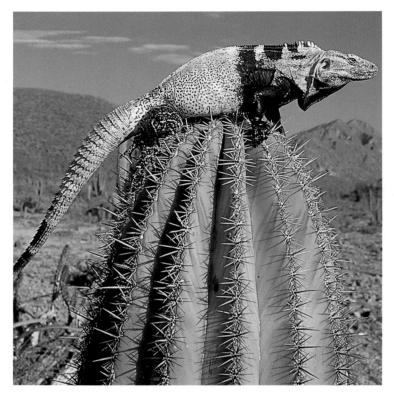

▲ **BLOOMING TASTY**

The San Esteban spiny-tailed iguana lives on an arid island in the Mexican Sea of Cortez, and eats cactus flowers and other plants. Iguanas are the main group of leaf-eating lizards, but there may be few leaves in arid habitats, and desert island iguanas often feed on the flowers and fruit of cacti and other water-retaining succulents.

◄ **SALTY FOOD**

The Galapagos marine iguana is the only truly marine lizard. Although its two Galapagos land iguana relatives have a rich diet of leaves and flowers, the male marine iguana must enter into the cold ocean to feed. Marine iguanas dive down 33 ft to feed on seaweed before returning to bask on the rocks. There is so much salt in their food that they have special glands in their nostrils to get rid of it.

▼ **FRUITY FEAST**

This little Barbados anole is enjoying a feast of bruised mango fruit. Feeding on fruit is a much easier option than eating leaves. Fruit is easily digested, and it provides much more energy than leaves. However, fruit is seasonal, so lizards that like to eat fruit have to eat other things as well, such as insects.

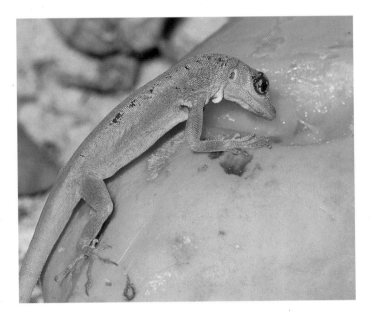

▲ **VEGETARIAN GIANT**

Although most monitor lizards are meat-eaters, one species eats fruit more than anything else. Gray's monitor lizard from the Philippines habitually swallows whole fruit and is the world's only plant-eating monitor lizard. It also eats insects, but fruit can make up almost 60 percent of its diet. Other lizards, including the iguanas and chuckwallas of the Americas, eat leaves. Digesting leaves requires a large, specialized gut with valves, to slow down the passage of leaves through the digestive system.

▼ **DRIED-OUT DIET**

Lizards living in very dry deserts have little green vegetation available to eat. They bulk up their insect diets by feeding on seeds in the dry season when insects are scarce. In the arid Namib Desert of southwestern Africa, the shovel-snouted lizard can survive on wind-blown seeds alone. It obtains not only its energy, but also all of its water requirements from this incredibly dry diet.

Did you know? Some lizards eat insects when young, then move to a diet of leaves as they get older.

Focus on the

The Komodo dragon, or Ora as it is also known, is the largest lizard in the world and the only one believed to include humans in its diet. The size of the dragon has been exaggerated, however—the maximum length for the dragon is not much more than 10 ft—and attacks on humans are very rare. The Komodo dragon is a type of monitor lizard that is confined to four small islands in Indonesia's Komodo group. It has one of the smallest geographical ranges of any of the large carnivores, and is classified as endangered. Komodo dragons feed mainly on large animals, such as deer, which they attack by ambush. Once it is bitten, the prey is doomed to die, even if it escapes. The Komodo dragon's saliva contains deadly bacteria that cause death by blood poisoning within a couple of days.

HUMAN PREY?
This is a view from Baron's Cross on Komodo Island. The Baron's Cross commemorates the Swiss naturalist, Baron Rudolph von Reding, who disappeared on the island in 1974, after he strayed away from his tour group. No one knows for certain how he died, but all that was ever found were his glasses and camera, on the hill where the Baron's Cross now stands.

IN THE TREETOPS
The first thing a newly hatched Komodo dragon does is run for the nearest tree and climb up it quickly. Young Komodo dragons live in the treetops for two years, to be safe from the adults who live on the ground. The young eat large insects, geckos, and skinks.

Komodo Dragon

FIRST TO ARRIVE

Komodo dragons have an extremely good sense of smell and they can detect prey from a long distance. This large adult dragon on Rinca Island has been attracted by the smell of a dead goat. The lizard has powerful jaws, and its muscular legs are armed with talonlike claws, allowing it to rip prey open and devour it very quickly.

THREE'S A CROWD

Two more, slightly smaller, dragons arrive. Soon after this picture was taken, a fight broke out. Eventually, the largest dragon took the goat by the head and started to consume almost the entire carcass, while the other two tore pieces of flesh off. Less than 20 minutes later, the goat had completely disappeared.

ARTIFICIAL GATHERING

In the past, park rangers used to attract Komodo dragons to a feeding station so that tourists could safely watch them. This practice is no longer carried out, since the dragons were becoming reliant on the handouts and were beginning to think of tourists as a source of food. The dragons now act naturally again and look for their own food.

Water for Life

▲ LAPPING IT UP

Many lizards drink by lapping up water with their tongues. This Madagascan day gecko has climbed down a tree in order to drink from a puddle. Northern Madagascar, where this day gecko lives, is a very wet region, with regular rainfall. For the majority of lizards, finding water to drink is not a problem.

Like all animals, lizards need water to survive. They obtain it in several ways, depending on the species and habitat. Many drink water from pools and puddles, or get it from dewdrops or condensed fog. Moisture can also be obtained from food. For some lizards, finding water is hard, and a few never drink at all. Lizards living in very dry places produce harder, drier droppings than those in rain forests, where water is plentiful. This helps them conserve water that would otherwise be wasted. Some lizards use water that is produced by their own bodies. "Metabolic" water is created when food is broken down within the body. A few desert-adapted specialists use this "metabolic water" so that they do not need to drink.

▲ WATERPROOF COAT

This Bell's dab lizard is basking in the sun. If an amphibian or mammal did this, it would lose a lot of water, either from its moist skin or by sweating, but lizards have tough, dry skin that keeps most water in. This is one reason why reptiles are so common in hot, dry places.

SHADY CHARACTER ▶

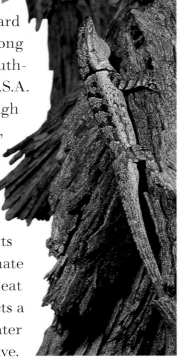

The ornate tree lizard lives on large trees along the riverbanks in south-western parts of the U.S.A. These trees have rough bark and broad leaves, which give lots of shade. Rainfall is rare, so the lizard must get all the water it needs from its insect prey. An ornate tree lizard has to eat seven or eight insects a day to get enough water to survive.

Stony Stare of the Basilisk

According to mythology, the basilisk's stare could turn people to stone or cause them to burst into flame. Also known as the Cockatrice or Royal Serpent, this mythological basilisk is shown as a type of dragon, sometimes as a snake-like creature, as in the novel Harry Potter and the Chamber of Secrets. *No one knows what the mythological basilisk looked like because anyone who saw one would never speak again! Real basilisks are harmless Central American lizards whose main claim to fame is that they can run across water.*

▲ DEVIL'S DEW

The thorny devil comes from the deserts of Western Australia, where it hardly ever rains. But the thorny devil's diet of ants does not provide it with enough water to survive. The lizard gets around this problem by drinking any dew that condenses on its body at night. The dew trickles down channels between its "thorns" and into the corner of its mouth.

◄ OUT IN THE SUN

The western brush lizard is closely related to the ornate tree lizard, but it lives in the sparse bushes and trees of the Sonoran Desert. With their small leaves and slender branches, these bushes offer little shade from the sun. The brush lizard loses much more water than the tree lizard, and must eat 11 or 12 insects a day to keep its water levels high enough.

▼ WATER FROM FAT

Some desert geckos, such as Australia's Kimberley fringe-toed velvet gecko, store fat in their tails to help them survive. This fat is mainly used to provide energy when food is short, but it can be broken down to make water. One gram of fat produces just over one gram of water.

Body Temperature

A lizard's body temperature depends on the temperature of its surroundings. Unlike birds and mammals, which produce their own body heat, cold-blooded lizards need to bask on hot surfaces such as sun-heated rock, or have warm air around them. In the hot tropics, lizards can be active day or night. Elsewhere, they need the heat of the sun to raise their body temperature. Most lizards speed up this process by basking in the sun, but they must be careful not to get too hot.

▲ ON GUARD

A lizard in the sun has to keep its eyes open for predators. Birds of prey are a particular threat to this African ground agama—the slightest shadow will send it dashing back to its refuge, a hole at the base of the bush. A basking lizard may look like a dozing sunbather, but it is usually alert.

▲ TOO HOT TO HANDLE

If you have ever walked barefoot on sand in the summer, you know how hot it can be. Desert lizards have to face this problem every day. The African ground agama gets around it by standing on the balls of its feet. Other species do a balancing act, standing on two feet with two raised before swapping over.

◄ SUN-POWERED COLOR

Some male lizards adopt very bright colors to attract a female. The male common agama is bright blue and red, but only during the daytime. At night, the sleeping lizard is much drabber and duller, but it quickly becomes more colorful as the day warms up. After a minute or so of basking in the sun, the lizard changes from gray to glowing red and blue again.

▲ BASKING IN THE RAIN FOREST

Not much sunlight reaches the ground in a rain forest, yet some lizards warm up by basking on the rain forest floor. When a rain forest tree falls, it creates a natural gap in the canopy, and a patch of sunlight appears on the ground. In tropical America, ameivas look for these sunny patches, and are usually the first lizards to arrive after a tree has fallen.

▲ WARM AT NIGHT

Lizards that hunt at night still need to be warm to be active. The granite night lizard from California spends the day in a rocky crevice, venturing forth to capture insects and scorpions only after dark. It manages to do this by seeking places where the rocks are still warm from the sun's rays. It is also able to remain active at temperatures too low for most lizards.

CATCHING THE RAYS ▶

So that they can get warm quickly, basking lizards flatten themselves to expose their bodies to the sun or the warm ground. They do this by expanding their ribs outward and making themselves more rounded. Some desert lizards are naturally rounded and can present almost half their body surface to the sun.

ON TIPTOES ▶

This northern desert horned lizard is round and flattened—the ideal shape for basking, since it can present a large surface area to the sun. When it gets too hot, it lifts its underside and tail off the sand. Horned lizards spend long periods of time almost motionless, waiting for the ants that they eat to swarm into reach.

Mating Time

In almost every lizard species, the male courts the female instead of the other way around. Male lizards go to great lengths to attract a mate and often put themselves in danger in the process. Some become bright-colored and others change their behavior, making themselves as obvious to predators as to females. Male lizards may even go without eating, since the urge to mate or defend a female overrides their hunger for food. Males of most lizard species will mate with more than one female if they get the chance. Very few lizards stay with one partner through a mating season, though some Australian shingleback skinks stay together for life. A few lizard species do not need males to reproduce, and females of these species produce offspring without needing to mate.

▲ GREEN NOD
Male green iguanas use the dewlaps hanging down from their chins to settle disputes about mating territories. The dewlap is green, but dominant males develop a paler-colored head and orange pigment on their shoulders. The dewlap draws attention to the signature bob display.

◄ WAVING A FLAG
Anole lizards are well camouflaged from predators, but have a trick that makes them obvious when they want to attract a mate. Anoles possess a bright-colored throat flag, or dewlap, which remains hidden until it is erected for display. Different species have different colored dewlaps, so that males do not attract females of the wrong species.

▲ PUTTING ON A SHOW

In many species of lizard, the males develop bright-colored skin to attract females during the breeding season. The European sand lizard is a good example, since the males sport bright green on the flanks in spring and summer, and the females remain gray-brown.

▼ TEST OF STRENGTH

If a visual display fails to deter a rival, some of the larger lizards, such as these Gould's monitor lizards, will resort to brute force. Fights between male monitors look aggressive as they rear up and try to grapple each other to the ground, but it is rare for either combatant to be injured. Instead, the defeated lizard will break away from the fight and run away.

◄ DANGEROUS LIAISONS

When a male lizard has courted a female and chased away any rivals, he will try to mate with her. In the early stages, he rubs his chin on her neck or nudges her until she lifts her tail and allows him to mate. Some animals, such as these Californian alligator lizards, may mate for a long time, so the female looks out for enemies.

VIRGIN BIRTH ►

Some lizards can produce offspring without mating. When this happens, the babies are identical clones of their mother. Lizards that can give birth without mating include the Indo-Pacific house gecko. Such species are good colonizers of islands, since a single arrival can start a colony all on her own.

Egg Layers

Most lizards lay eggs, but a significant minority, particularly in colder climates, give birth to live young. Although most egg-laying lizards lay eggs with soft, leathery shells, some geckos lay eggs with hard shells like those of birds. Few lizards show interest in their eggs or young, generally leaving after laying or giving birth. Some larger species, however, such as iguanas and monitor lizards, may guard the nest site for a short time after laying. Baby lizards are independent from birth or hatching. As soon as they are born, they face a wide range of predators and few juveniles survive to adulthood.

▲ SPOTTED MOTHER

Leopard geckos inhabit grassland from Iran to India. A female leopard gecko can breed at the age of two and continue to breed for 14 years. Females lay two leathery-shelled eggs one month after mating. A female may produce eight clutches (16 eggs) in a year, and potentially produces over 160 eggs in her life.

◄ BEFORE LAYING

Eggs can be seen in the body of this female house gecko. Most lizards lay eggs rather than give birth to live young. Geckos have clutches of just one or two eggs. Pale areas in the gecko's neck contain a substance called calcium carbonate, which is used to strengthen the eggshell before the eggs are laid.

INDEPENDENT BABY ►

Hatchling leopard geckos are 3–3½ in long and have a much bolder ringed pattern than adults. During its first few days, the baby survives on its absorbed yolk reserves. When these reserves run out, it starts to hunt for insects.

SOFT-SHELLED EGGS ▶

The eggs of most lizards have soft, leathery shells, and they are vulnerable to drying out, so they are usually laid in moist sand or soil. Hatching lizards break out using a small "egg tooth" in the front of the mouth, which drops off soon after the lizard has hatched. This newly emerging collared lizard will survive for days on the absorbed contents of its yolk sac before it needs to hunt insects.

◀ MAKING A BREAK FOR IT

Unlike the hard-shelled eggs of most other geckos, leopard gecko eggs have leathery shells. After 6–12 weeks the infant gecko is ready to hatch. It cuts a small hole in the eggshell using a small egg tooth on the front of its jaw. Once it has absorbed the last of the yolk from its yolk sac and learned to breathe using its lungs, it breaks out of the shell.

Did you know? A baby lizard's egg tooth drops off soon after it has slit a hole in the egg and hatched.

HARD PROTECTION ▶

Tree-living geckos, such as the gold dust day gecko, lay just one pair of eggs. The moment they are laid, they are soft and can fit into crevices in bark or on walls, sticking to both surfaces and the other egg. The eggs harden quickly when they come into contact with the air, giving the developing babies protection from drying out.

Birth and Hatching

Some species of lizards lay eggs and others give birth to live young. Female lizards that give birth carry their offspring for less time than a female that lays eggs. Most lizards in warm climates lay eggs, but those living in colder habitats, such as Scandinavia, Patagonia, and Tasmania, usually give birth to live young. Such females can protect their young. They can seek out the sun and avoid enemies until the babies are ready to be born. When they are born, the mother rarely takes care of them. Whether they are born or hatch from eggs, the juvenile lizards exist for a while on nutrients absorbed from the yolk sac, but they must soon become predators of insects and other small animals, or they will be eaten by larger creatures than themselves.

▲ **LIVE YOUNG**
About one in five lizard species give birth to live young. The babies are born wrapped in thin, transparent sacs, from which they soon escape, taking a first breath in the process. Many live-bearing lizards live where it would be too cold for eggs to incubate. The common lizard has live young and lives as far north as Scandinavia inside the Arctic Circle.

◀ **PROTECTIVE MOTHER**
Only one lizard guards its young, the Solomons monkey-tail skink. Females usually give birth to a single infant, which never strays far from its mother and seeks shelter underneath her if it is threatened. Since the skink is a plant-eater, it is important that the baby eats some of its mother's droppings to get the microbes needed for it to digest leaves.

▲ GIVING BIRTH

Adult common lizards mate from March to June, depending on their location. The embryos take up to three months to develop inside the female, and she gives birth to a single litter between July and September. The average size of a litter is seven or eight, but large females may give birth to up to 11 offspring. The babies are born in a membranous sac, from which they escape within seconds. In warmer parts of the world, the common lizard may lay eggs. All baby common lizards have an egg tooth, even those that are born rather than laid in eggs.

Beware of Lizards

Iguanas might look cute when they are small, but these little green lizards can grow to six feet in length. All iguanas need to have special lighting and follow a special diet if they are to keep healthy. When they are three years old, male green iguanas may become quite aggressive in the breeding season, biting and using the tail as a whip. Female iguanas often become eggbound in captivity because they have not been allowed to mate and lay eggs. An eggbound lizard may die. You should never buy a lizard on impulse or because it looks cute. Even baby Komodo dragons look cute—but they have a nasty bite.

Did you know? Green iguanas guard their eggs to stop others digging them up and laying their own.

▲ FAST WARM UP

Baby common lizards are just under 1½ in long. They are independent from birth, and must find their own food and avoid numerous predators if they are to survive to adulthood. In Britain, newborn common lizards are much darker than adults. They may even be black, a color that helps them warm up faster in the sun, in order to hunt and be alert enough to avoid getting captured.

Lizards Under Attack

Snakes, birds of prey, and mammals, such as mongooses and meerkats, are all enemies of lizards, and they are capable of catching even the most alert, fast-moving species by day and night. More unusual predators include other lizards and various large invertebrates, including spiders, scorpions, and centipedes. Many predators are opportunistic and include lizards as only part of their diet. But others are more specialized and regularly prey on them—snakes in particular. Lizards have evolved all sorts of ways of escaping from predators, but the main reason that they survive as species is that they are simply so abundant. A single lizard can have dozens of offspring in a lifetime, and only a few of those offspring have to survive long enough to breed for the species to continue.

▲ STRENGTH IN NUMBERS
A single army ant would be a small snack for most lizards, but a swarm of army ants is another story. These fierce insects march across the rain forest floor in South America and overpower anything that gets in their way. Most of their prey is made up of other insects, but sometimes they kill and eat small lizards, too.

◄ EIGHT-LEGGED ENEMY
Invertebrates are animals without a backbone. Many species of lizards feed on invertebrates, but sometimes large invertebrates turn the tables and make the lizards their prey. In many parts of the world, arachnids, such as scorpions and large spiders, hunt and kill small lizards. This wheel spider is eating a web-footed gecko that it has caught along the dunes of southwest Africa's Namib desert.

◄ EATING EACH OTHER

A few lizards specialize in eating other lizards. For example, the slender pygopodid snake-lizards are specialist predators of skinks. In the deserts of North America, small spiny lizards are the main prey of larger lizard species. Here a black-collared lizard has caught a spiny lizard that was basking among the rocks.

CAUGHT UP IN THE COILS ►

A huge number of snakes prey on lizards and some feed on very little else. The common Asian wolf snake is one species that specializes in hunting lizards. Active at night, often inside houses, it will search underneath baskets, boxes, and boards for small lizards, which are then grabbed and constricted before they are eaten. This wolf snake has a house gecko in its coils.

◄ DEATH FROM ABOVE

A few birds, such as secretary birds and the kookaburra, specialize in killing and eating snakes and lizards. Many other birds, including this black-shouldered kite from Namibia, will eat any basking lizard that is not paying attention to the threat from the skies. Small lizards are swallowed head first and whole, and larger ones are torn apart by beak and claw to be eaten in chunks.

STRAIGHT FOR THE HEAD ►

The reptile-eating habits of some mammals are well known. Meerkats are small members of the same family as the cobra-killing mongooses. Smaller than a mongoose, the meerkat feeds on roots and small animals, including lizards. The meerkat's long canine teeth makes eating lizards easy, especially since the head is targeted first.

113

Defense Methods

Many lizards are small and looked upon as food by other animals. To escape being eaten, lizards have evolved a wide array of defensive mechanisms. One of the most effective is simply being well camouflaged and staying still to avoid detection. When this fails, the lizard may have to adopt a more active method of defending itself. Running away, diving off a branch, or even gliding to freedom are all simple escape procedures. But many lizards have evolved more elaborate defensive behavior, including displays intended to intimidate or confuse potential predators. Some of these are among the most extreme seen anywhere in the animal kingdom.

▲ BOLD DEFENSE

The toad-headed agama of Iran and southern Russia puts on a bold defense display. When it is threatened, it raises its front, opens its mouth wide, and extends flaps at both sides to make it look threatening. It then hisses, waves its tail like a scorpion, and jumps toward its enemy.

◄ PUTTING ON A SHOW

The Australian frilled lizard's first reaction to danger is to open its mouth wide to spread its neck frill. All of this makes the lizard seem suddenly less like an easy meal and more like a large, dangerous opponent. If this display fails to scare a predator, the lizard turns tail and runs, the frill trailing around its neck like a partially closed umbrella. The frilled lizard uses its display to scare rivals as well as predators.

THREATENING DISPLAY ▶

The shingleback skink from Australia tries to frighten predators by opening its mouth and sticking out its bright blue tongue. These lizards have short legs so they cannot run away, and must stand their ground. The rolling tongue, combined with a flattening and curving of the body, and a hiss, is enough to intimidate most animals.

▲ SEEING RED

The horned lizards of Mexico and the U.S.A. have one of the strangest defense mechanisms of any animal—they squirt foul-tasting blood from the corners of their eyes. They use this defense only against large predators. Birds and rodents are usually chased away by the lizard's prickly spines.

▼ CHAMPION WRESTLER

Monitor lizards have powerful jaws, which can deliver a painful bite. They use their tails as whips, dealing rapid blows to their enemies. When the argus monitor is threatened, it makes itself look bigger by standing on its hind feet and inflating its throat. If this fails, it attacks, wrestling fiercely until its opponent flees.

▼ FIGHTING TINY ENEMIES

New Guinea's green-blooded skinks have a pigment in their blood that makes it bright green. This is thought to be a defense against the tiny blood parasites that cause a disease called malaria. Lizards suffer from seven types of malaria. The skinks' blood is believed to be so toxic, the malarial parasite cannot survive.

Did you know? The frilled lizard can run on its back legs at speeds of more than 12½ mph.

115

Color and Camouflage

A lizard's color is usually dictated by the habitat in which it lives: most desert lizards are sandy brown, most tree-living species are bark-colored or green. By matching themselves to the color of their background, they become well camouflaged, which protects them from animals that want to eat them. Some lizards take camouflage one step further and actually look like objects from their surroundings. Color is also important socially. Many male lizards adopt bright colors in the mating season, or change color or expose bright parts of the body when confronted by a rival.

▲ DEAD LEAF

Not all chameleons are green or camouflaged like living leaves. The West African pygmy chameleon lives in low vegetation in forests and is a drab brown with a series of darker lines making it look like a dead leaf. When the pygmy chameleon feels threatened, it just falls to the forest floor and lies still, disappearing among the leaf litter.

◄ WOODEN PERFORMANCE ►

Chameleons are not the only lizards capable of changing their pattern or color. The Malagasy flat-tailed gecko can also alter its appearance—here it matches the wooden planks of a hut (left) and the bark of a tree (right). By combining camouflage with a flattened body edged with thin fringes of skin, this nocturnal gecko can sleep unseen during the day. Its gripping toes mean that it can merge into the background on vertical surfaces or even the undersides of branches. At night, it wakes up again to feed.

▲ LEGS LIKE STICKS

The Sri Lankan kangaroo lizard has legs that look like fine twigs, and body and head patterns that look like a dead leaf or fern frond. When a predator approaches, the kangaroo lizard skips quickly across the forest floor and then disappears into the dead leaves. It is often found near forest streams, and can run across water.

Omen of Evil
Chameleons are considered evil omens in Africa, but nowhere are they feared as much as on the island of Madagascar, where the giant panther chameleon is avoided at all costs. Drivers who would not think twice about hitting a dog or a chicken swerve to avoid chameleons, preferring to risk a serious accident rather than incur the wrath of an angry spirit. Chameleons are also believed by some Malagasy people to be poisonous, so they are never handled or eaten, even when other meat is scarce.

◄ SPOTLIT SIDES

In 1938, a British naturalist captured a small, cave-dwelling lizard in Trinidad and reported that it had white spots on its flanks that glowed like a ship's portholes. Recently, a male lizard was caught, and the 1938 report was proved correct. The purpose of the spots is unknown, but it is thought they might be used to startle predators.

STANDING OUT ▶

Four-fingered skinks are usually brown and blend in with the leaf litter, but this individual is an albino. Being born an albino can make life more dangerous. Albinos lack colored pigment and stand out from their surroundings, making them easy targets for predators. Not only are they more likely to be eaten, they are also thought to be vulnerable to sunburn.

Focus on

The beaded lizard and the Gila monster are the world's only venomous lizards. They are found from southwestern U.S.A. through western Mexico to Guatemala in Central America. Both feed on eggs, fledgling birds and newborn rodents, such as rats and mice. Since they do not need venom to deal with such harmless prey, the lizards' poison is mainly for defense. They hang on when they bite, forcing more venom into the wound. The poison causes great pain, but there are no records of people being killed by these lizards.

RIVER MONSTER

Named after the Gila River, where it was first encountered by settlers, the Gila monster is a spectacular lizard. Its rounded head is covered in large, studlike scales a little larger than those on its body. Bulges in the rear of the powerful lower jaw indicate the position of the bulbous venom glands.

NO RELATION

It was once thought the Gila monster and beaded lizard might be related to snakes. But the snake has its venom glands and fangs in the upper jaw, while the lizard's venom teeth are in the lower jaw of its skull. This means venom has evolved in these lizards separately from its evolution in snakes.

BEADED BEAST

When it is seen close up, the beaded lizard is easily distinguished from its northern relative. It is less colorful than the Gila monster, and its yellow and brown skin camouflage it well. Its head is longer and more squarish, and the neck is longer. The beaded lizard, so called because of its beadlike scales, is larger but less aggressive than the Gila monster.

Venomous Lizards

VENOMOUS WARNING

When it feels threatened, the Gila monster opens its mouth like a large blue-tongue skink. But the Gila monster has more to back up its threat than most lizards. Its bite is not only painful, but can result in a venomous bite bad enough to require urgent medical attention.

DESERT DWELLER

The Gila monster is most at home in saguero cactus desert. Its bright pink and black warning colors send out a clear message to potential predators, "Mess with me at your own risk." It may look sluggish, but the Gila monster can move remarkably quickly.

WHERE DO THEY LIVE?

Found in the southwestern U.S.A. and northwest Mexico, from Utah to north Sinaloa, the Gila monster spends much of its life underground, hunting in rodent burrows. It is rarely seen except at dusk or after nightfall.

AT HOME IN THE WOODS

The beaded lizard lives in woodland and scrub in Guatemala, west Mexico and south Sonora. With a longer neck, tail and legs than the Gila monster, it can reach almost 3 ft. Although it is in the main a ground-dweller, it can climb trees.

Human Threats

Wild lizards are threatened by humans in many varied ways. People collect and kill them for their meat, their skins, their eggs, and their internal organs. They are also caught to be sold as pets, particularly the rarer and more exotic species. Many lizards are killed out of fear—chameleons and geckos are considered devils in some cultures, for instance. Many lizards die simply because they make the mistake of looking for insects on a busy road. Less obvious threats include habitat destruction and the introduction of new predators, such as cats and rats. Island lizard species are particularly vulnerable to introduced predators, since they usually have only small populations and may be found nowhere else. Other introduced animals, such as goats, may destroy lizards' habitats, leaving them with nowhere to live.

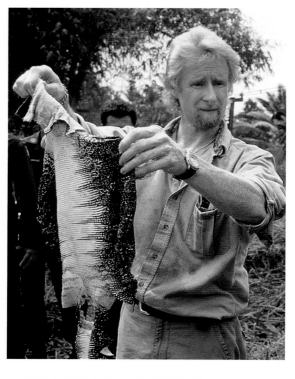

▲ KILLED FOR FASHION

This monitor lizard skin was found by the author when he joined a police raid on a large illegal factory in Asia, in which wild reptiles are killed and skinned in huge numbers. Lizard-skin handbags, shoes, belts, and coats are still popular fashion items. The police found bags of skins from monitor lizards and pythons, and rescued and released live reptiles.

◄ CAUGHT FOR THE POT

Tribal rain forest people have always eaten reptiles and other animals. Such small-scale hunting does no real damage, but when hunters start supplying markets in the towns, it becomes a serious problem. These green iguanas are alive but in shock. Keeping them alive means that their meat stays fresh for the customer.

▲ HABITAT DESTRUCTION
Tropical rain forests have been shrinking for many years due to "slash and burn" farming and clearance of trees for timber. The result is huge loss of habitat and the disappearance of many forest species.

▲ GORY SOUVENIRS
Although endangered species are protected by international laws, in some countries they can still be found for sale to tourists. This shop is selling stuffed monitor lizards, pythons, and cobras, reptiles that are all becoming very rare in the wild. Buying this type of souvenir may lead to the buyer being prosecuted when they return to their own country.

▼ TERRIBLE CONSEQUENCES
Introducing destructive animals to a new place can have catastrophic results. When the brown tree snake was introduced to the island of Guam, it began eating the native geckos, skinks, and flightless birds. Now the lizards are very rare and most of the flightless birds have become extinct.

▲ DANGER ON THE ROAD
Lizards cross roads to hunt, find mates, or move to new areas. Many, such as this Namibian flapneck chameleon, are too slow to get out of the way of cars. The death toll in some areas is huge. Near many busy towns, wildlife has been almost wiped out.

121

Conservation

Individual species can be protected and so can habitats. Conservation means all the ways there are of protecting and taking care of wildlife for the future. Breeding endangered species in captivity is an important part of conservation, as is the education of people in places where animals are threatened. The education of young people is very important, because one day they will be the decision-makers with the power to decide what happens to threatened species. Conservation also involves fighting against illegal trade and the smuggling of animal skins, meat, and live reptiles for the pet trade.

▲ TAKING CARE OF THE LAND

There is no point in protecting a species if the habitat in which it lives is not also protected. Unique habitats such as this heathland often contain species found nowhere else. If the habitat is threatened, the species may become extinct. Many habitats are destroyed and their species lost before anything has been done to save them.

▼ CAPTIVE BREEDING

One way to help endangered species is to breed them in captivity. The monkey-tail skink was threatened in its native Solomon Islands, so zoos in the U.S.A. and Europe began breeding them in captivity. Researchers have learned a lot about these lizards, and the unusual maternal behavior of the females. Populations built up in projects like this can be used to provide animals for reintroduction into the wild in the future.

▲ PROTECTIVE PENS

Conservation usually involves fieldwork. Biologists on Komodo are monitoring the hatching of baby Komodo dragons. They must catch all the hatchlings just after they emerge from the nest. The metal screening around the nest protects the dragons.

CENTER FOR LEARNING ▶

Education is an important part of conservation. If people do not know about animals, they are less likely to care if they become extinct. Education helps people to see how interesting their local wildlife is. This center in England tells people about British reptiles. Wildlife can also be valuable—Komodo islanders earn their livings from tourists who come to see the dragons.

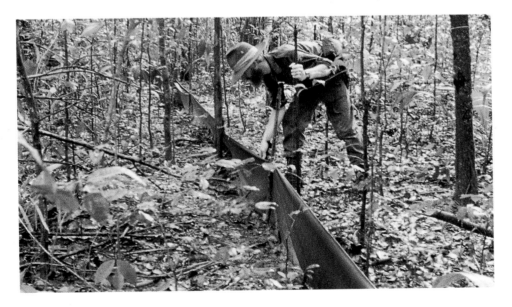

◀ KEEPING TRACK

Baby Komodo dragons have been captured and are being weighed inside a little cage. A few of them will be fitted with radio-tracking devices so that researchers can follow their daily activity in the forest once they have been released. The dragons spend the first two years of life in the trees and without transmitters it would be impossible to find them, let alone follow them.

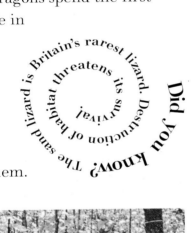

Did you know? The sand lizard is Britain's rarest lizard. Destruction of habitat threatens its survival!

DRIFT FENCE ▶

Many lizards live in leaf-litter and the top layers of soil. Drift fences are used to capture burrowing lizards. They come to the surface at night after rain and bump into the fence. Then they travel along it and fall into buckets buried along its length. By looking at what ends up in the buckets, scientists can find out which species live on the forest floor.

GLOSSARY

albino
An animal that has no color on all or part of its body but belongs to a species that is usually colored.

amphisbaenian
A legless reptile that has evolved from the lizards.

arid
Very dry.

bask
To lie for hours in the warmth of the sun, like a person who is sunbathing.

bifurcated tail
A V-shaped tail that is formed when one tail does not fully come off and a second tail then grows from the wound.

billabong
Branch of a river that comes to a dead end in a backwater or stagnant pool.

bird of prey
A predatory bird with sharp claws and a hooked beak, such as an eagle or falcon, that hunts animals.

camouflage
Colors or patterns that help an animal blend into its surroundings.

canine
A sharp, pointed tooth next to the incisors that grips and pierces the skin of prey.

carcass
The dead body of an animal.

carrion
Animals that have been dead for some time.

carnivore
An animal that eats only meat or fish.

clutch
The number of eggs laid by a female at one time.

cold-blooded
An animal that does not produce its own body heat, but maintains the temperature range needed by basking or sheltering, depending on the temperature of its surroundings.

colony
A large group of animals of the same species living together.

conservation
Protecting living things and helping them to survive in the future.

crocodilian
A member of the group of animals that includes crocodiles, alligators, caimans and gharials.

crustacean
A type of invertebrate such as crabs, slaters or woodlice.

dewlap
A flap of skin under the chin, often brightly colored and used for display.

diaphragm
A sheet of muscle separating the chest cavity from the abdominal cavity, the movement of which helps with breathing.

diapsid
A type of skull with two openings on either side, behind the eye socket.

digestion
The process by which food is broken down so that it can be absorbed into the body.

digit
Finger or toe.

dinosaur
An extinct group of reptiles that lived from 245–65 million years ago.

dominant animal
An animal that the other members of its group allow to take first place.

eardrum
Part of the ear that vibrates when sound hits it.

egg tooth
A small tooth in the front of a baby lizard's mouth, or a sharp point on the tip of a baby crocodilian's snout, used for breaking out of the egg.

endangered
A species that is at risk of becoming extinct.

epidermis
The outer layer of the skin.

estuary
The mouth of a large river where it reaches the sea.

evolution
The process by which living things adapt over generations to changes in their surroundings.

extinct
When every member of a species of animal or plant is dead.

gall bladder
A small organ attached to the liver.

gastroliths
Hard objects, such as stones, swallowed by crocodilians, that stay in the stomach to help crush food.

gator
A shortened name for an alligator, commonly used in the USA.

gizzard
A muscular chamber in an animal's gut that grinds large lumps of food into small pieces or particles.

habitat
The type of place where an animal naturally lives.

hard-tongued lizards
All lizards not contained in the group Iguania.

herbivore
An animal that eats only plants.

hibernation
A long period of inactivity when all body processes are slowed down in very cold weather.

Iguania
The name given to the group of lizards containing iguanas, agamas, chameleons, anoles, swift lizards, lava lizards, basilisks and spiny lizards.

incubation
Using heat to help eggs develop.

infrasounds
Very low sounds which are too low for people to hear.

intestines
Part of an animal's gut where food is broken down and absorbed into the body.

invertebrate
An animal without a backbone.

Jacobson's organ
A sensitive organ in the roof of the mouth into which the tongue places scent particles.

juvenile
A young animal before it grows and develops into a mature adult.

keratin
A horny substance that makes up the scales of lizards, snakes and tuataras.

mammal
An animal with fur or hair and a backbone, which can control its own body temperature. All female mammals feed their young on milk.

Marine
Sea-living or sea-going.

membrane
A thin film, skin or layer.

microbes
Living things such as bacteria too small to be seen with the naked eye.

molar
A chewing and grinding tooth at the side of the jaw.

nictitating membrane
A third eyelid that can be passed over the eye to keep it clean or shield it.

omnivore
An animal that eats plants and other animals.

osteoderms
Rigid plates that add strength to a lizard's skin.

palate
The roof of the mouth. An extra or secondary bony palate separates the mouth from the breathing passages.

parasite
A living thing that lives on or inside another living thing and does not benefit its host.

pigment
Colored matter in the skin.

poaching
Capturing and/or killing animals illegally and selling them for commercial gain.

pod
A group of young crocodilians just out of their eggs.

predator
An animal that hunts and kills other animals for food.

prehensile
Able to grip.

prehistoric
Dating from long ago, before people wrote down historical records.

prey
An animal that is hunted and eaten by other animals.

pupil
The dark opening in the middle of the eye that allows light to enter.

rainforest
The tropical forest that grows near the Equator, where it is hot and wet all year round.

range
The maximum area in which an animal roams.

reptile
A scaly, cold-blooded animal with a backbone. Reptiles include lizards, snakes, crocodilians and turtles.

rodent
An animal such as a rat, mouse or squirrel with chisel-shaped incisors (front teeth) used for gnawing.

salivary gland
Gland opening into or near the mouth that produces the fluids in the mouth that start the process of breaking food down for digestion.

scavenger
An animal that feeds on carrion.

scutes
The thick, sometimes bony, scales that cover the bodies of some lizards and crocodilians.

slash and burn
Cutting down and burning forests to create farmland.

sloughing
Shedding skin. Lizards slough when a new layer of epidermis has grown underneath the old skin.

solar panel
An electric device that turns heat and light from the sun into electric power.

species
A group of animals that share similar characteristics and can breed together to produce fertile young.

succulent
A plant that stores water in its stem or leaves.

swamp
A waterlogged area of land or forest, such as the mangrove swamps that are found in Florida, USA.

territory
An area of land that one or more animals defend against members of the same species and other species.

tropics
The hot regions or countries near the Equator and between the Tropic of Cancer and the Tropic of Capricorn.

tuataras
Lizard-like animals that have their own separate reptile group. Today there are only two living species in New Zealand.

venom
Poisonous fluid produced by two lizards, the Gila monster and the beaded lizard, to deter predators.

vertebrate
An animal with a backbone.

viviparous
Giving birth to live young rather than laying eggs.

vocal cords
Two folds of skin in the throats of warm-blooded animals that vibrate and produce sound when air passes through them.

warm-blooded
An animal that is able to maintain its body temperature at the same level all the time.

windpipe
In air-breathing animals, the breathing tube that leads from the mouth opening to the lungs.

yolk
Food material that is rich in protein and fats, which nourishes an embryo inside an egg.

INDEX

PICTURE CREDITS

b=bottom, t=top, c=centre, l=left, r=right